PARENTS AND ADOLESCENTS LIVING TOGETHER

Part 1: The Basics

PARENTS AND ADOLESCENTS LIVING TOGETHER

Part 1: The Basics

GERALD R. PATTERSON, PH.D.
MARION S. FORGATCH, PH.D.

Castalia Publishing Company
P.O. Box 1587
Eugene, OR 97440

Copyright ©1987
by Castalia Publishing Company
10 9 8 7 6 5 4 3

ISBN 0-916154-16-5
Printed in the United States of America

Copies of this book may be ordered from the publisher.

Editorial and Production Credits
    Editor-in-Chief: Scot G. Patterson
    Copy Editor: Cheryl Brunette
    Editor's Assistants: Evelyn Levine and Jody Kishpaugh
    Layout: John Macioce
    Cartoons by Cheryl Reed
    Cover Photograph by Evelyn Levine
On the Cover
    Jody Kishpaugh, Miles Kishpaugh, and Scot Patterson

Contents

Acknowledgements vii
Preface ix
Introduction: The Importance of the Family
    as a Social Unit 1
Chapter 1: Teaching Compliance and the
    Readiness to Be Socialized 21
Chapter 2: Using Requests that Work 39
Chapter 3: Monitoring and Tracking—
    The Basics for Involved Parents 61
Chapter 4: Teaching Through Encouragement 97
Chapter 5: Setting Up Point Charts 129
Chapter 6: Discipline
    Unit 1 161
    Unit 2 179
    Unit 3 203
Chapter 7: Family Processes—Slow Changes,
    Dramatic Outcomes
    Unit 1 227
    Unit 2 251
Glossary 273
Appendices 277
About the Authors 283
Order Forms

Dedication

This book is dedicated to families—our own, those of our friends, and especially the hundreds of families with problems —all of whom had so much to teach us.

Acknowledgements

This book was a gleam in the eye of the publisher before either author took pen in hand. In the process of writing and rewriting, the lines differentiating authors and editor became fuzzy. In a very real sense the existence of this book is as much a function of the publisher and editor, Scot Patterson, as it is of the authors. It is a family book about families.

We gratefully acknowledge the two decades of support for the research underlying the principles described. The National Institute of Mental Health section on crime and delinquency provided grants making it possible to work through many of the complex problems inherent in the study and treatment of families.

Finally, it must be said that this book could have been written by any of our clinical colleagues, John Reid, Patricia Chamberlain, and Kate Kavanagh. Each of them contributed a great deal of their clinical knowledge to the thinking reflected in this book. Hopefully, each of them will write books for parents and professionals that put this book out of date. This book reflects neither the first word nor the last word on the subject of helping families change. Rather it describes a set of ideas that are in passage.

Preface

This book has been written to help parents manage the problems they typically encounter when their children reach adolescence. Even parents who have had very little trouble raising their children find that new problems arise during the teenage years. This is a difficult time for parents, and for children as well. It is a transition period when children go through rapid changes. Adolescents are no longer children, and yet they aren't quite adults. They vacillate between expressing their own individuality and being dependent on their parents. They can drive cars and demand increasing degrees of freedom. Parties are no longer a time for simple games and talking—now there is drinking and the use of drugs to contend with. These experiences are difficult to handle, and parents often become concerned about their adolescent's ability to make wise choices. Parents living with adolescents are confronted with new issues on a regular basis, and these issues must be *negotiated* with the adolescent instead of being decided by decree.

Parents need to know how their adolescents are doing so they can steer them away from trouble and encourage them to develop their talents and interests. But parents must be careful when they intervene or their efforts will be met with obstinance and resistance. We have written this book because parents often need help sorting out the complicated issues they face when their children become teenagers. Parents also need effective techniques for producing lasting changes in adolescent problem behaviors, and some ways to control the negative emotions which often accompany the struggles between parents and teenagers. Perhaps one of the most difficult challenges is achieving a good balance between protecting adolescents from serious trouble, while giving them enough freedom to try out new experiences. The techniques outlined in this book are designed to help parents maintain this balance without turning their households into battlegrounds.

This book draws on our experience as parents, researchers, and clinicians. Between us we have raised five children, all of whom are now beyond their adolescent years. We are also researchers who have devoted our professional careers to studying families (30 years for Jerry, 15 for Marion). Our work has focused on building a comprehensive framework for understanding the processes that operate within families, and helping troubled families change. The results of our studies, and those of our colleagues doing similar work, have been discussed in professional books and journals, but most of the concepts are so new that they are not covered in the literature currently available to parents.

Both of us are members of the Oregon Social Learning Center (OSLC), which is a research facility staffed by a group of scientists and clinicians who are dedicated to strengthening the American family. The studies carried out at OSLC are relatively unique in that they are concerned with real families who are dealing with problems and situations very much like yours. The purpose of this research is to design treatment approaches for families whose problems have gotten out of control. This blend of science and therapy has many practical implications for families. Our research indicates, for example, that parents in nondistressed families have specific family management skills that parents in disrupted families don't seem to have. When we teach these family management skills to parents who are having difficulties with their teenagers, problem behaviors decrease dramatically. The two books in the *Parents and Adolescents Living Together* mini-series describe these family management principles in detail so that parents can live in harmony with their adolescents.

The research at OSLC has involved more than 1,000 families with children ranging in age from toddlerhood to adolescence. We have studied all kinds of families: "intact families," where the father and mother are the biological parents of the children; "step-families" where there are two parents, only one of whom is a biological parent of the children; "blended families," where both parents in the family have children from previous relationships; "adoptive families," where the parents adopt children; and "single-parent families," where the children live with only one of their parents, often the mother, usually as the result of separation or divorce.

During the last two decades, social learning investigators have spent hundreds of thousands of hours conducting field studies in homes and classrooms across the country. What is being studied is the simple idea that people change as a result of the interactions they have on a daily basis with one another. (The historical context of social learning theory is discussed in more detail in Appendix 1). Before these studies were undertaken it was always assumed that interactions changed people, but no one could figure out just how it worked, or even how to study it. For some reason it took social scientists a long time to come up with the idea of going into the real world to see what is going on in family life.

In our studies, we examine the family from many different perspectives: we ask parents and children (separately) about their experiences; we go into homes and record the behavior of family members as they interact with one another; we call parents and children on the telephone and ask them what is happening on a daily basis; in the laboratory, we ask families to sit down and talk about their problems and we study how they do that; we ask teachers to tell us how children behave in the school, and we talk to classmates as well. The families involved in our research studies share large chunks of their family life with us. Much of the information in this book has been derived from our contacts with them.

The clinical work at OSLC focuses on changing antisocial and aggressive behavior in children. This covers a wide range of problem behaviors such as disobedience, arguing, tantrums, school problems, fighting, lying, stealing, shoplifting, burglary, assault, truancy, and substance abuse. Helping families with extreme problems has made the processes that disrupt families more dramatic and easier for us to see. We have found that the best way to help adolescents with these problems is to teach their parents how to change behavior. This almost invariably involves changing the parents' behavior as well as the adolescent's.

Some parents are disappointed when they find out how much effort it takes to make the necessary changes. They would rather have a professional do it for them, magically and with ease. Unfortunately, that doesn't work. Parents are in the best position to help their adolescents because parents control the resources that motivate them. Parents also determine whether or not the family environment is constructive and healthy. Perhaps the most compelling reason of all is that parents are the ones who love their children enough to make the commitment necessary to socialize them and protect them from harmful experiences. For these reasons, it is necessary for parents to be actively involved in changing problematic adolescent behaviors.

The general approach in this book is to teach parents how to be consistent in applying common sense techniques. If the problems your family is experiencing are relatively mild, this book should provide the information you need to smooth out the rough edges. Families involved in long-standing or intensely angry struggles with one another may not, however, be able to change what is going on by simply reading this book. In that case, you should seek out a counselor, a psychologist, or a professional family therapist to help you make some of the necessary changes. It is very difficult for parents in severely distressed families to turn things around without some professional assistance and support. Parenting can be intensely rewarding when everything is going well, but it can be equally frustrating and demoralizing when things get out of hand. We hope you can use the information in this book to make your family living experience one that is filled with love, joy, mutual respect, and a spirit of cooperation.

How this Book Is Organized

The first two chapters of the book present several key concepts that are the foundation for understanding family dynamics. The first chapter presents two related ideas—"the readiness to be socialized" and the issue of teaching compliance. The second chapter offers some guidelines for using requests that work. These concepts provide the background for understanding the material that follows in the next four chapters. We think it is best for parents to read through the chapters in the order they are presented.

The next four chapters (Chapters 3, 4, 5, & 6) provide practical information that will help you to make significant changes in the way you relate to your adolescent. The confrontations, the daily battles that repeat themselves over and over again, and the yelling and screaming can be stopped by using the techniques outlined in these chapters. It is a detailed account of the family management procedures we have developed as the result of our research. Chapter 3 discusses the importance of monitoring your children, or "seeing the big picture." This chapter also describes tracking, or paying attention to the details of your adolescent's behavior. Chapter 4 introduces the concepts related to teaching your children through positive means, such as using attention and praise. Chapter 5 shows parents how to set up point charts for dealing with chores and behavior. This provides the structure for creating a contingent home environment. Chapter 6 gives parents the tools they need to stop unpleasant behaviors by using discipline techniques that work. There is so much material in this chapter that it has been divided into three "units," each with its own homework assignment.

Chapter 7 addresses the question "How is it that perfectly well-intentioned parents end up having problem children?" The answer is that things often change slowly in families, and because the changes are so gradual they can easily go unnoticed. The *processes* contributing to these changes are made up of tiny events that happen on a day-to-day basis. These events may at first seem insignificant, but they can produce dramatic outcomes that bring misery to everyone in the family. The term "coercion" is introduced as a way of describing some of the destructive processes that operate within families. The side effects of misusing punishment are also discussed. This chapter has been broken down into two "units."

These are all common sense techniques, but most people

have difficulty the first time they actually try to apply them. We talk about the mistakes parents often make so that you can avoid critical pitfalls. A number of problems that are common to families with adolescents are used as examples. Chapters 2-7 also contain some "teaching dramas" describing families "doing it right" and "doing it wrong." The characters and the situations are composites of the families we have been in contact with—our own, our friends, and our clients. The names and many of the details have been changed. Cartoons have also been added to help illustrate important ideas.

How to Use this Book

Parents who are using this book on their own should work through the chapters one at a time. It is recommended that you start at the beginning, and read the chapters in the order in which they appear. Each chapter (except Chapter 7) ends with a homework assignment. These assignments have been designed to help you put into practice the principles described in the chapter. The assignments build on one another so it is important not to skip any of the chapters and to complete all homework assignments.

Although we have tried to avoid using specialized language in this book, some psychological terms are unavoidable. New terms are defined as they are introduced. For easy reference, a glossary appears at the back of the book. If you forget what a particular term means, flip back to the glossary for a quick reminder.

The references that appear at the end of each chapter have been selected to give students, mental health professionals, and highly motivated parents some resources for further study.

We would like to hear from parents about the kinds of problems they are having with their adolescents. Please write to us in care of the publisher and let us know how things are going. Are you having trouble implementing the programs outlined in this book? What do you like/dislike about the material we have provided here?

Use by Students and Professionals

It was mentioned earlier that the *Parents and Adolescents Living Together* mini-series is primarily for parents, but it is also intended for psychology students and mental health professionals. The material presented here is less technical than the information available in the professional literature, yet it provides a state-of-the-art understanding of important social learning concepts that is not available anywhere else. Students may be reading this book as part of their course work in psychology, social work, or counseling programs. (It should be particularly revealing for younger students in that it presents the other side of the coin—that is, what it's like to be a parent.) It should also be very useful as an introduction to "social-interactional psychology," which is an area of investigation and theory-building that is just emerging.

Professors using this as a text in courses might want to consider changing the order in which chapters are assigned. For example, Chapter 7 on family processes might be assigned first. We have moved it to the end of the book because the material is conceptually difficult and will impede parents who are looking for techniques that will help them change problematic adolescent behaviors. The chapter is, however, one of the most important chapters in the book.

About Part 2

Part 2 of the *Parents and Adolescents Living Together* mini-series builds on Part 1. We would like to encourage parents to begin with this book because it offers an introduction to key concepts that is not included in Part 2. In the second book, we assume that you have worked through the homework assignments in Part 1. When used together, the two books give parents all the skills they need to guide their children through adolescence.

The first section of Part 2: *Family Problem Solving* focuses on communication and describes how to work on family problems by setting up highly structured family meetings, or "family forums." Additional procedures are outlined for managing sensitive issues with a minimum of conflict. In the second section of the book, three issues are addressed that concern parents of adolescents and mental health professionals: teaching sexual responsibility, controlling drug and alcohol use, and academic achievement.

If you are interested in Part 2, or want to order additional copies of Part 1, several order forms are provided at the end of this book for your convenience.

INTRODUCTION

The Importance of the Family as a Social Unit

During the centuries when technology changed very slowly, the family was a social unit that remained relatively static. The extended family was at the center of most people's lives, and each new generation raised their children in much the same way. Grandparents were intimately involved in helping to raise the grandchildren, which insured continuity. The basic values about work, play, and the importance of forming good relationships with others changed very slowly.

The Problems Faced by Modern Families

Today, however, social and technological changes are taking place within decades instead of centuries. Unfortunately, as the pace of change has accelerated, there has been a breakdown of the central family. Most families are no longer embedded in a protective and caring network of relatives and

1

friends that endures for a lifetime because about one family in five moves every year. The extended family no longer functions as a vehicle for imparting basic values to each successive generation. This task is left to the parents, who often find themselves attempting to raise a family without adequate support.

But this is not the only problem experienced by modern families. Studies indicate that about one-half of all recent marriages are likely to be shattered by divorce. This has resulted in the emergence of several new family configurations such as "blended families" where the children are from more than one marriage, and "single-parent" families where one adult is trying to raise the children (studies also indicate that single-parent families are "at risk" for a host of problems including out-of-control children [1]). New trends in the work force are also creating problems for families. For most of history, the function of one parent was to provide while the other parent cared for the children. Now both parents work at least part time in almost 40% of all families. The overall trend evident in these changes is that parents have less time to care for their children, and less support in their role as parents.

Loss of support, divorce, and spending less time with children gradually take their toll on the well-being of the family. These are all stressors that make it difficult for parents to be effective caretakers. In the face of these stressors, it takes good parenting skills to keep the family from falling apart.

The advent of television is another factor that has changed the way children are raised. The average person in our culture watches television two to three hours each day. This means a significant part of our waking reality is spent immersed in a fantasy world created by someone else. The problem with this is that the programming geared toward children contains an alarmingly high rate of violence and

2

interpersonal aggression. Television is a powerful medium, and children are receptive to the messages it provides about basic values and the rules of society. The several hundred studies summarized by the National Institute of Mental Health leave little doubt that the antisocial behavior so graphically depicted on TV increases the antisocial behavior of the children who watch it.(2) In addition to promoting violence as a means of solving problems, television also tends to paint unrealistic pictures of family life, with the seamy side shown on the soaps and the silly side on the sitcoms. Only a few programs, like the Bill Cosby Show, depict parents realistically struggling with the daily problems of family life. Parents should take a position on what children are allowed to watch on television because television affects the basic values and behavior of children. Recent studies also show that the amount of time children spend watching television is negatively correlated with academic performance. In other words, the more television they watch, the lower their scores on achievement tests.

These changes have put tremendous pressures on the family. Cultural values about what is good, what is important, and the role of the family seem to shift with the tides. As parents, we are caught in the ebb and flow of these changes. We are told, directly and by innuendo, that some of the values we want to teach our children are no longer important because they are "old fashioned." This is the era of the expert, the specialist, and it is implied that parents should leave the teaching of their children to persons better qualified. We are told to stand aside with our horse-and-buggy values, and make room for the "here-and-now" generation. Cool has replaced committed. The question children are asking is no longer "How can I contribute to the family?", but "What's in it for me?"

The influence of hormones, the values embraced by the peer group, and the mobility afforded by cars all contribute

3

to the urgency with which adolescents express their need to "do their own thing." Our job as parents is to help adolescents blend the superficial fads with old-fashioned moral values by "nudging" them in the right direction (if you "push" them, they will often reject your input). This means parents must be prepared for the fact that teenagers will undoubtedly try out some aspects of the new values such as hair styles, but this is not a problem as long as they don't reject the best parts of the old values such as the importance of working and loving.

Our rapidly changing culture, our knowledge of our own shortcomings, and the rule testing our teenagers subject us to support the argument that we should live for the here and now. These self-doubts and ambiguities also tend to keep us off balance when we are trying to negotiate the Teenage Trinity: sex, drugs, and the use of the family car. What is fair? What is safe without being overly restrictive? How can you arrive at a compromise everyone can live with? When do you compromise, and when do you just say *no*? How do you say *no* and make it stick? What are other parents doing about these things? These are some of the questions that parts one and two of this mini-series will attempt to answer.

We believe that the fundamental basis for "the good life" is being able to balance self-interest with a sense of responsibility, and having the skills necessary to form enduring relationships with others. These things can only be taught within the family. Even before children come in contact with their peer group and professional educators, the family is preparing them for the experience. If parents are not successful in establishing their children's basic readiness to learn, then the efforts of experts, teachers, and well-meaning adults who are willing to teach them essential skills will be wasted.

As authors, we see it as our obligation to provide modern parents with two things that we believe will strengthen their position in meeting these responsibilities. First, we offer information about what other parents and adolescents actually do. This information gives parents an opportunity to develop their own positions on the key issues that come up when living with adolescents. We do not feel, however, that having information or taking a position is enough. It is also necessary to know how to *change* behavior—your own behavior and that of your adolescent. As you have probably already discovered, it is when you try to change behavior that you are most likely to run into trouble.

One of the things that makes family living and raising children interesting is the fact that everyone is changing almost imperceptibly over time. If you try to ignore the changes then the peer group, teachers, and other outside influences will determine how your children change. A better option is to become an integral part of the change process so that you have some control over the way things turn out for your children. That is what this book is about—how parents can be constructively involved in these changes.

Working, Playing, and Loving

For the majority of adults, happiness depends upon how well work and family relationships are going. Laughing and playing together make it easier for family members to work, and to relate to one another. Extensive surveys of our culture leave little doubt that these continue to be central issues.(3) Acquiring and maintaining each of these skills is difficult; to achieve a good balance among all three (relationships, work, and play) is something we all strive for, yet rarely accomplish. Most parents probably already know this. But what is needed in addition to this awareness are some strategies to use when your children are deficient in any one of these skills.

As parents we often find ourselves in the position of defending the ancient values regarding the importance of good family relations and learning how to work because we know at a deep level that these values will serve as anchor points in the lives of our children. Our children love to play and want to be free to do what they want. As they grow older, adults must ask them to spend less time playing so they can begin contributing to the family, and this can easily become a source of conflict. Parents must also spell out the rules for *earning* increasing degrees of freedom, rather than just offering it with no strings attached. Taking this position can also produce trouble—children tend to assume that freedom is part of their Bill of Rights. But as adults we know freedom is something that must be earned. Giving freedom regardless of what children do can create problems in the long run (we will discuss this topic in more detail later in the book).

The Importance of Work

One way to earn freedom is to demonstrate responsibility in the world of work. The work assigned to teenagers usually involves household chores, school assignments, and sometimes a job outside the home. Responsible adolescents also make an effort to contribute to the quality of family living. They show a certain amount of self-discipline with respect to their schoolwork. At home, they usually pull their share of the load and sometimes, without being asked, they notice extra help is needed and volunteer. Sensitive parents encourage such responsible behavior with increased privileges, attention, or a mixture of both.

The Importance of Play

At the same time, we know that play is extremely important. It keeps our spirits from becoming weighed down by responsibilities, and allows us to return to work with renewed vigor. Play time provides an opportunity to relax and leave our cares behind. One of the axioms in our own family is, "When you work hard, you need to play hard." It may seem odd that it is necessary to express this, but many adults (and teenagers too) fall into the trap of taking life too seriously; they are absorbed by their work and the responsibilities of daily life, and they forget how to play. This can take the joy out of life. It also makes it difficult to give your best performance at work or at school.

Play also helps us to keep our relationships loving, cooperative and happy. Play makes an important contribution to our mood and is good medicine for a variety of ills such as depression, discontent, boredom, anxiety, and disillusionment. Jerry, the co-author of this book, kept a record of the variables related to life satisfaction (including working, playing, and loving) for 365 consecutive days. His data indicated that if we went longer than two weeks without playing together for two or three days, his mood plummeted, and so did his ratings of our relationship! Having fun and laughing together builds a healthy bank account to draw on when times are difficult.

Playing together is important for adult relationships and for adult/adolescent relationships. When parents find it necessary to punish adolescents, they need to have some credits built up in their bank accounts because as adolescents grow older they must *choose* to accept the punishments their parents hand out. That is one of the big differences between dealing with younger children and managing the behavior of adolescents. You cannot force your will on an adolescent. You may win for the moment, but when they are away from home they can (and will) have their way. That is one of the reasons it is so important to have fun together as a family.

The Importance of Loving

Children learn how to love by having good relationships with others. The first lessons are imparted by parents as infants and young children learn how to relate to them.

Later, other people become involved in teaching children how to build good relationships in which love can grow. These are important lessons for future adjustment and life satisfaction—a world without love is a barren place.

But love is a fragile thing. Stress tends to tear apart the good relationships that are the basis for love, especially when more than one person in the family is under fire. Bad moods accompanied by sarcasm and angry reactions are the result of too much stress. This creates a smog of unpleasantness that impinges on everyone, and the family suffers. If one person is up when another is down, that person can comfort or soothe the other's pain. But if everyone is having trouble at the same time the tendency is for one person to snap, then the other person snarls, and pretty soon there's a dogfight that gets the whole pack involved. Fighting in this way is not healthy, and we believe that good relationships are destroyed by this. Once it starts, the process is difficult to change. Everyone gradually becomes involved, and when one person identifies an area needing change, the rest of the family rigorously defend their positions. Families become disrupted when the people in them are unable to request or make changes. Strategies for minimizing conflicts and enhancing the process of making constructive changes in families are discussed at length in this book as well as the next.

Achieving a Good Balance Between Work, Love, and Play

Most of us continue to struggle as adults to achieve a good balance between work, love, and play. Yet we often fail in our own relationships, work too hard or lose our jobs, and many of us give up playing altogether. Sometimes adolescents can help their parents regain their balance by exposing them to new music or the latest dance steps, and encouraging them to try other experiences they once enjoyed. The teaching that goes on in families is not a one-way street. The exchanges you have with your children change them, and you as well.

More than ever, our culture needs good people. To endure, a society must have adults who can, when necessary, sacrifice self-interest in order to love and work cooperatively with others. As we shall see, the family provides the critical first step in teaching children how to do this. If the family fails in this responsibility, it has not been shown that the omission can be rectified by experts, no matter how many university degrees they have earned.

The Readiness to be Socialized

One of the prime functions of the family is to get children ready to be socialized by the major forces outside the family. This means that children must be taught by their parents to respond appropriately to the people around them, and be willing to learn from others. There is a fundamental sense in which adolescents cannot learn what teachers, the peer group, or others have to teach them unless their parents have specifically prepared them for the experience. We also believe that a sense of self-worth goes along with this openness. Learning new things should be rewarding for children. It is important for them to seek out new challenges rather than passively waiting for things to happen to them. But parents must prepare children for this by teaching them to be receptive to instruction. Children who do not have this readiness avoid or run away from learning experiences, and they are disrespectful to those who try to teach them.

The idea of preparing children to be socialized does *not* mean that parents should teach them to be equally responsive to everyone and everything around them. At the same time that children are prepared to be receptive to others, they should be encouraged to adopt a consistent set of values to guide them in their choice of who will influence them outside the home, and what the direction of those influences will be. The readiness to be socialized does *not* imply being passive. We believe that what happens at home determines the kinds of experiences and peers that children select for themselves outside the home. They tend to feel comfortable with people and situations that match what they have learned at home. There are many children who live in ghettoes who have been taught by their parents what and whom to select in the neighborhood. These youngsters do not become delinquent even though they are seriously "at risk." Once your children have selected the right people and situations, or they have been selected by others (it does work both ways), then they must be ready to learn. If children haven't been socialized at home to be receptive to this learning, then they will miss many of the opportunities to grow and learn from the positive influences around them.

Love: A Necessary, but Not Sufficient Ingredient

Some writers suggest that the primary function of the parent is to provide love. In one way, they are right. It is true, for example, that most of the children brought to clinics for psychological treatment receive very little love from their parents. But this picture is missing some important pieces. We have identified some things that come up in ordinary human relationships with spouses, friends, and adolescents that turn love off (this is described in Chapter 7). It is important to know what these things are.

Love is the keystone of being a good parent, but it is *not* enough. There are times when you must say NO, and you will not be loved for doing this. It is an act of love to take an unpopular position which, in the short run, causes you to have conflicts with your adolescent. It is *not* appropriate to let your teenager get in the car with someone who has a reputation for getting drunk, driving like Mario Andretti, and having accidents. If anything ever happened to your adolescent because you didn't have the energy to say "no," you would never forgive yourself. Teenagers don't always have the self-control or foresight to be objective about what they are doing, and it is your job to step on the brakes when you see trouble ahead. If you have established a healthy bank account with your teenager, your relationship will not change dramatically because you said "no." Many teenagers are, in fact, grateful to have the excuse that they can't do something because their parents won't permit it.

Using discipline and keeping your children out of trouble are not the whole picture either. In order for family members to be close to one another, they must have the feeling that people genuinely care about them. There must be a certain amount of "unconditional positive regard." Even though they sometimes make mistakes, so do you. But this doesn't mean you don't love each other anymore.

Adolescents

What is unique about raising adolescents? Most of the comments made so far apply to raising children of any age, but we believe that parents encounter a new set of problems when their children become adolescents. In raising young children, the roles of parent and child are reasonably distinct. Parents make the rules and choose the directions for growth. During preadolescence, parents discuss the rules and offer a rationale for why they are important; but in the last analysis, the rules are not particularly negotiable. With young children, rule setting is *not* an affair carried out among equals. It is up to the parents to establish rules in a firm but loving way. The field studies carried out in the last decade at Berkeley very clearly lay to rest the idea that it is good for children to be raised in permissive or egalitarian environments.(4) These studies and others have found that socially competent children come from homes where the

11

rules are clear and firmly enforced, and the parents provide a rich supply of love.

Adolescents, on the other hand, are almost equals but they are not quite competent enough to be left entirely on their own. They have strong ideas, at least as definite as your own, about what the rules are and what they should be. By late adolescence, parents must be willing to give their teenagers increasing amounts of input in the rule-setting process. Otherwise it is very difficult to enforce the rules, since older adolescents spend so much time without adult supervision.

Fortunately, studies have consistently shown that adolescents generally endorse *most* of their parents' basic values and beliefs. *But* they are also buying into the values of their peer group. It is here, in fact, that adolescents have a new card to play. They can point to changes in the times and claim that, "All of my friends are allowed to. . . ," "None of my friends have to. . ." and so on. We have given parents some ammunition to use during these confrontations by including information about what parents with normal adolescents allow. If you still have some unanswered questions, ask other parents what they are doing.

Another difficulty experienced by parents who are trying to manage the behavior of adolescents is that teenagers are like chameleons. One day they behave with wisdom and maturity beyond their years, and you think of them as responsible young adults. The very next day they show poor judgment, or act as silly as a 10-year-old, and you feel discouraged. This movement back and forth makes parents wonder if their adolescents are making any progress at all. Will this child ever become reliable?

It is important to recognize that the flip flop from adult to childlike behavior is confusing to adolescents as well. This stage of life is full of ups and downs. Adolescents are subject to startling hormone changes that come and go with accompanying fluctuations in mood. One day they are energetic, happy, and affectionate. The next day they angrily barricade themselves behind their bedroom doors, emerging when they must, scowling. They burst into tears or throw temper tantrums for no apparent reason. Adolescents tend to see the world in back and white (gray is not in fashion during the teen years). Even the words they use express the extremes of their experiences—always/never, awesome/gruesome. They are reactionaries who seem to say just the opposite of what their parents want them to say. Reasonable requests are often met with "no," before they have even had a chance to hear them. Successful experiences make them feel superhuman; then they throw their parents aside and proclaim their independence. When they fail at something, you can hear the hot air escaping as they shrivel before your eyes like a balloon with a fast leak; at these times they need their parents to pump them up again. This seesaw state of affairs makes adolescents worry that they have a Jekyll & Hyde personality. Their fears about being "normal" cover a vast array of issues: sex, the clothes they wear, the length and color of their hair, and the possibility of rejection by peers. Their once beautiful complexions erupt with neon pimples that three coats of blemish cream cannot hide; yet this is the very time when they are painfully aware of their appearance. Is it any wonder they have trouble keeping it all together?

What makes all of this such a problem is that parents need to get adolescents ready to *leave home*. They are supposed to be preparing for independence, the world of work, college, serious relationships, and the other responsibilities inherent in adult life. They are also supposed to be Zen masters in their handling of drugs, sex, alcohol, and cars. It is a little like trying to teach someone how to survive in an avalanche. You hardly know where to begin.

It is easier when they are 10 years old. Then you can simply take the position that they are not ready for sex, alcohol, drugs, or staying out late at night. All parents would agree with this position, which means there is very little to discuss. But what do you do when they are 15 or 16 years old? By then your adolescent may have some knowledge of, and experience with, the opposite sex; *but how much is too much*? If there are some aspects of dating and intimacy that you feel they are not ready for, what do you do? They undoubtedly have had some experience with alcohol and drugs (90% do by the end of high school), but *how much* should you allow?

Where do you draw the lines for someone who is getting ready to leave home? That is the question. Every parent takes a slightly different position on where that line is. One of the purposes of this book is to let you know where other parents draw the line, but the final decision is yours. Given that you have your position well in mind, how do you negotiate these agreements with your adolescent? How do you get the agreement to work?

As parents, we have the distinct impression that we are the gate keepers of three doors. There is one door marked NO that we stand in front of; it leads to experiences we believe our adolescents are not yet ready to handle. After they leave home they may seek out these experiences, but that will be up to them. Right now, it may be our opinion as parents that they are not ready. We know that some things, such as drugs and alcohol, represent the first stage in a process that can easily get out of hand. It is our job as parents to prepare our adolescents for these experiences so they can deal with them when we are not there. This is one sense in which adolescents really are *not* our equals. We know about long-term consequences that adolescents tend to overlook (drug addiction, car accidents, unwanted pregnancies, sexually transmitted diseases, the whole dreary litany). We use that knowledge when we take our position in front of the door marked NO.

There is another door marked YES. We are not too con-

cerned about the experiences behind that door. We can allow our adolescents to do things like going to school dances and staying up a little later in the evening without much worry. The third door is labelled BY NEGOTIATION. This means that parental permission is required before the adolescent is allowed to engage in the experiences behind the door. Before opening the door, however, the parents and the adolescent must discuss the rules together and arrive at some kind of

15

consensus. After this is done, the door is open for them to walk through as a potential equal. Use of the car and experimenting with sex are two good examples of things that must be negotiated before adolescents are given access to them. Saying no or opening the door can be painful for parents, but it is necessary to learn how to do both.

Perhaps you feel that we have taken something simple and made it so complicated that only an expert would find this material to be of interest. Many of the books for parents suggest that learning to communicate clearly with adolescents is all that is required. Others will tell you to be more warm and loving. Still others suggest throwing teenagers out if they won't shape up. It is perhaps a disappointment to find that there is no one simple solution. Being warm, providing discipline, and communicating clearly are all important, but you must also know how to change behavior—your own and that of your children—to be successful as a parent. There are clearly defined techniques presented in this book that you can use to improve the relationships in your family.

What we propose here is not simple, and it will not be easy to implement. But we know that the principles outlined in this book are effective in helping families to change for the better. We have taught hundreds of disrupted families, with problems much more severe than the ones you are probably experiencing, to use these same principles. With professional supervision, three out of four families who came to our research center for treatment were able to change the behavior of their children so that it was within the normal range.(5)

Just so you don't feel alone as parents, we have included a piece of history, a father's tirade against his ungrateful, disrespectful, lazy son. What makes this lecture so interesting is the fact that it was *carved* into stone tablets 3700 years ago in ancient Sumeria.(6) It begins with the father asking the eternal question that all parents with teenagers must ask, followed by a typical adolescent response.

"Where did you go?"

"I did not go anywhere!"

"If you did not go anywhere, why do you idle about?"

Sound familiar? So does the rest. In spite of the passage of time and all the changes that have taken place since then, the modern reader cannot fail to feel the father's bitterness and frustration as he lashes out at his teenage son.

"Come now, be a man. Don't stand about in the public square, or wander about the boulevard. When walking in the street, don't look all around. Be humble and show fear before your teacher. You who wander about in the public square, would you achieve success? Go to school, it will be of benefit to you. Because of your clamorings, yes, because of your clamorings—I was angry with you—yes, I was angry with you. Because you do not look to your humanity, my heart was carried off as if by an evil wind. Your grumblings have put an end to me, you have brought me to the point of death. I never sent you to work, to plow my field. I never sent you to work to dig up my field. I never sent you to work as a laborer. 'Go, work and support me,' I never in my life said to you. Others like you support their parents by working. But you, you're a man when it comes to perverseness, but compared to them you are not a man at all. You certainly don't labor like them—they are the sons of fathers who make their sons labor, but me—I didn't make you work like them. I, night and day am I tortured because of you. Night and day you waste in pleasures."

So don't feel dismayed or alone in your struggle through the adolescent years. The time will pass all too quickly and you will be standing at the door blinking back the tears, watching your adolescent leaving home.

It would be a mistake to present only the parents' point of view in discussing the struggle through adolescence, because our children also suffer. One thing adolescents have in

17

common is the strength of their feelings. Can you remember, even just a little, how judged, controlled, and misunderstood you felt in your teen years? Most adolescents develop an overwhelming desire to cast off the shackles of parental control. This becomes an obsession when they are almost ready to leave home. Adolescents often feel attacked or put down when their parents attempt to give them corrective feedback. In their desperate quest for independence teenagers find themselves wishing for absolute freedom. They look forward to the time when their parents no longer make the rules.

The next excerpt, which was found in a prominent position in the bedroom of Marion's 16-year-old goddaughter, illustrates this point.

ANARCHY

"To be governed is to be watched over, inspected, spied upon, directed, legislated at, regulated, docketed, indoctrinated, preached at, controlled, assessed, weighed, censored, ordered about, by men who have neither the right, nor the knowledge nor the virtue. To be governed means to be at each operation, at each transaction, at each movement, noted, registered, controlled, taxed, stamped, measured, valued, assessed, patented, licensed, authorized, endorsed, admonished, hampered, reformed, rebuked, and arrested. It is to be, on the pretext of the general interest, taxed, drilled, held for ransom, exploited, monopolized, extorted, squeezed, hoaxed, robbed. Then, at the least resistance, at the first word of complaint, to be repressed, fined, abused, annoyed, followed, bullied, beaten, disarmed, garotted, imprisoned, judged, condemned, deported, flayed, sold, betrayed, and finally, marked, ridiculed, insulted, dishonored. Such is government, such is justice, such is morality."

Pierre-Joseph Proudhon
Courtesy of Bound Together Book
1369 Haight St, S.F.,CA. 94117

To be closely watched and found lacking would be extremely painful for anyone, but this is especially true for adolescents. In this book and the one to follow we suggest that you watch over your teenagers very carefully. We also take a strong position that children need consistent discipline when they behave inappropriately. On the other hand, if you focus *only* on what they do wrong, they will feel "admonished, hampered, reformed, rebuked, and arrested." It takes a certain amount of skill and a lot of love to see the potential in that diamond in the rough. Diamond cutters are aware of the imperfections they must chip away, but their primary goal is to emphasize the assets of the stone so that the finished product is a glittering, multifaceted work of art. This is the task that faces you as a parent—chipping away the undesirable aspects of adolescent behavior while encouraging growth in positive directions.

Introduction References

1. Bloom, B. L., Asher, S. J., and White, S. W. "Marital Disruption as a Stressor: A Review and Analysis." *Psychological Bulletin, 85,* 867-894.

2. Pearl, D., Bothlet, J., and Lazar, J. (Eds.) *Television and Behavior: Ten Years of Scientific Progress and Implications for the 80s.* Washington, DC: U.S. Government Printing Office, 1982.

3. Campbell, A., Converse, P., and Rodgers, W. *The Quality of American Life.* Russell Sage Foundation, 1976.
                                See Also
   Bradburn, N. M., and Caplovitz, D. *Reports on Happiness.* Chicago: Aldine Publishing Company, 1965.

4. Baumrind, D. "Parental Disciplinary Patterns and Social Competence in Children." *Youth and Society,* 1978, 9, 239-272.

5. Patterson, G. R. "Beyond Technology: The Next Stage in Developing an Empirical Base for Parent Training." In L. L'Abate (Ed.) *Handbook of Family Psychology and Therapy*, Volume 2. Homewood, IL: Dorsey, 1985.

6. This piece of history was introduced to us by Dr. Raymond Montemayor. It was taken from Kramer, S. N. *History Begins at Sumer: 39 Firsts in Man's Recorded History*. Philadelphia: University of Pennsylvania Press, 1981.

CHAPTER 1

Teaching Compliance and the Readiness to Be Socialized

Socialization is the process of teaching children the rules of society and how to respond appropriately to the people around them. Children are *gradually* socialized during the hundreds of thousands of interactions they have with parents and other people. It is through these interpersonal exchanges that children learn subtle social skills such as empathetic listening, turn-taking while talking, sharing, caring for the feelings of others, and cooperation. These high-level skills, which must be patiently shaped and molded by parents, are critical for developing relationships with other people. Well-socialized children know how to behave appropriately. They tend to follow rules, are socially responsive, and are generally liked by their peers. Children who do not learn these skills are socially handicapped.

Teaching Compliance During the Early Stages of Socialization

Sometime between the ages of two and 12 most parents

teach their children the complex social skills that replace the toddler's approach to social situations. Very young children use mildly unpleasant behaviors to get what they need until they learn more acceptable ways. When they are upset with something in their environment, they fuss and cry and sometimes have full-blown temper tantrums. This is one of the few ways infants can let their caretakers know they need to be fed or their diapers need to be changed. These responses are unpleasant to others, but they are good ways for infants to express their discomfort and get immediate attention from their parents. Many unpleasant behaviors, such as temper tantrums, are part of our genetic wiring—they do not have to be taught. For example, blind children who have never seen a temper tantrum know exactly what to do.(1) It is normal for children to use these behaviors in the beginning, but by the age of six months parents should very gently start to teach them other ways to communicate their needs. There are many ways to satisfy needs and express frustrations that are less unpleasant to others.

In order to learn these other ways of interacting with people, young children must be taught to be reasonably compliant. The concept of compliance relates directly to the child's willingness to follow rules, to be receptive to learning new behaviors, and to act in a cooperative spirit. It is difficult to teach noncompliant children anything. It takes them more learning trials before they acquire new skills, which means these youngsters tend to be less competent than their more cooperative peers. Some parents fail to teach their children to be reasonably compliant, and this has a profound effect on the course of the child's development. Researchers are currently investigating the possibility that children who are making normal progress can be distinguished from children who later become antisocial or delinquent as early as two or three years of age by looking at measures of compliance.

Children who are generally compliant are in a good position to acquire new skills. When directions are given, compliant youngsters listen carefully so they can carry them out. The questions they ask tend to be "how" rather than "why." "Why" questions are important, but they are not always appropriate (does a child really need to know *why* it is necessary to take out the garbage?). When compliant children understand what is expected of them, they set out to accomplish the task at hand. Compliant children also respond to corrective feedback. New skills are gradually acquired and refined through the process of following instructions and receiving feedback. Adults also acquire and refine skills through this same process.

Problems Experienced by Noncompliant Children

Noncompliant children receive very few of the benefits that socialization, or the learning process described above, have to offer. When they are given instructions, they focus their attention on what is *wrong* with the directions, rather than putting their effort into carrying them out. They argue about insignificant details, and seem to enjoy foiling the person giving the directions. They get so caught up in this game of disrupting things that they repeatedly miss opportunities to take the many small steps required to learn a new skill. This is why noncompliant children tend to be incompetent; it is also part of the reason they are unpopular. No one likes to be defeated by an incompetent nitpicker.

But the problems experienced by noncompliant children don't stop here. These children also avoid responsibility. When they are asked to help out, they respond by having temper tantrums. This unfortunate combination of behaviors—noncompliance, temper tantrums, and avoiding responsibility—sets the stage for an unhappy future. We call this set of behaviors the "antisocial triad."

23

When Things Fall Apart: The Antisocial Triad

When we talk about socializing children we are referring to the process of replacing the antisocial triad with more acceptable behaviors. This process takes place so slowly it is almost impossible to tell that it is happening.

Parents tend to be highly selective about the course and timing of this training. For example, some parents require their children to complete chores or homework assignments, but they are willing to tolerate occasional temper tantrums. Other parents never permit temper tantrums, but they accept several reports of truancy before they become concerned. Some parents allow their adolescents to act like they have a chip on their shoulder, responding irritably to others and pushing against rules whenever they encounter them. Such parents often regard this kind of primitive noncompliance as a special kind of independence, or even a sign of latent creativity.

Antisocial triad adolescents are not sensitive to what is going on around them, and they find it difficult to fit in when they are in a new setting. Studies of younger uncooperative children show they pay little attention to what other children or adults are doing.(2) Our hunch is that they are more tuned-in to their own behavior than to the behavior of others. Because of their generally nonresponsive approach, antisocial triad children receive very few of the benefits of the socialization process.

In order to learn from their experiences, children need to be sensitive to what other people are doing in different situations. Most settings have their own built-in rules for what is appropriate and what is not. The rules for acceptable behavior in the hallways at school, for example, are very different from the rules that apply in the classroom. These rules are generally well known to the adults and children who must coexist in these settings. It is important for children to learn to discriminate among settings, and to be able to change their behavior accordingly. They need to approach new situations with an eagerness to learn the implicit or explicit rules, and a willingness to abide by them. Well-socialized adolescents carefully track what other people are doing in new settings so they can learn the rules quickly and "fit in" without making waves.

Most of the problems experienced by antisocial triad adolescents in settings outside the home start out with noncompliance. When the teacher says, "Open your books and turn to page 17," these children ignore the request. They also avoid routine homework assignments by simply "forgetting" their books. Classroom rules are ignored as though they only apply to everyone else. These adolescents talk out in class and disrupt their classmates. In fact, they spend so little time working that they also learn very little, which is why they tend to fail at academics. When corrected, they talk back to the teacher or have mini temper tantrums.

Antisocial triad adolescents can always rationalize their behavior. Why should they worry about what other people are doing? Other people are stupid anyway, and what they are doing is not worthy of attention. Classroom rules are ridiculous, and the teachers are so old that they're probably senile. Incidentally, it is our experience in working with antisocial triad adolescents that lectures by parents, teachers, or counselors will not change the stories these children tell themselves about what is going on around them. By using the procedures outlined in this book, however, both the behaviors and the stories can be changed.

Antisocial triad children tend to receive less positive attention and praise than other children, and they also appear to respond less to what little they do receive.(3) The studies completed so far don't tell us very much about this, or how it happens. However, some studies have demonstrated that when children are placed in a noncontingent environment, the effectiveness of contingent praise is reduced (this is described in detail in Chapter 4). If children are given praise no matter what they do, then praise becomes meaningless. It is counterintuitive that praising children regardless of what they do creates an environment that is destructive to them, but this seems to be the case.

Criticizing children regardless of what they do also has dire consequences. What this does is to teach children to stop trying. Why should they extend themselves if they receive the same reaction from their parents regardless of their performance? Negative comments delivered randomly by an angry parent can damage a child's sense of self-esteem and make it difficult for the parent to bond with the child.

Consequences for Others

In addition to learning less from their environment, antisocial triad adolescents profoundly alter it. They generate a smog of irritability (that is, testy or hostile behavior) wherever they go. All it takes to start a new conflict is a simple request. For example, if you ask your adolescent three times to take out the garbage, the third request is likely to be delivered with a certain amount of hostility. A hostile affect is one of the few things antisocial triad children do notice, and they usually respond in kind. The next thing you know, you're in the midst of a major confrontation. After a dozen or more such confrontations about taking out the garbage you learn that it is easier to do it yourself. It takes 30 *seconds* to take out the garbage, but it takes 30 *minutes* to recover from the argument that was necessary to get your teenager to do it. These repeated confrontations with parents and other adults actually teach the adolescent to respond in an irritable manner when asked to do something. They avoid responsibility in this way, but they also lose their popularity. Research studies have consistently shown that family members tend to get what they give. Those who are hostile and irritable in their interactions with other family members tend to receive the same treatment in return.(4)

Observation studies show that there is tremendous pressure on parents of antisocial triad children to issue continuous commands and requests. In fact, *any* adult dealing with such a teenager is likely to become involved in this "command/noncomply" game. Teachers at school are forced to become command machines, issuing demands at a high rate to get unsocialized children to do what the others do willingly. This makes the noncompliant adolescent a target for anger and rejection by adults everywhere. Noncompliant children end up being referred for treatment when adults realize they are unable to help them grow.

Adjustment Problems for Antisocial Triad Children

Our studies of normal children show that antisocial triad behaviors interfere with learning the skills necessary for developing relationships with peers and academic performance. When children are noncompliant, have frequent temper tantrums, and consistently avoid responsibility, they tend to lack social skills and fail at school. Even when parents are successful at reducing antisocial triad behaviors, it has *not* been shown that social skills and academic performance automatically improve as a result. These children can be taught to read and do arithmetic, but it is difficult for them to catch up with the achievement scores of their classmates who have been making consistent progress all along. They also have trouble developing the subtle interpersonal skills that are necessary to be accepted by their peer group.

At this time, we simply do not know what the "catch up" margin is. When children are two years behind, are they destined to be permanent failures in the critical areas of academic and social skills? What if they are four or six years behind—what is the chance they will be able to catch up then? Current research has shed very little light on these questions, although there are studies in progress which should provide some answers. We do know, however, that the longer parents wait to socialize their children, the worse the prognosis is for their future adjustment and life satisfaction.

We do not mean to imply that antisocial triad children are destined to become maladjusted adults. Far from it. For example, only about one-half of the *extremely* antisocial third- and fourth-grade boys we have studied go on to become delinquent adolescents. Obviously, some families are able to change the course of events for their children. The data available so far indicate that it is the child who is both extremely antisocial *and* socially unskilled who is most at risk for becoming a chronic delinquent. But the fact that all problem children do not go on to become delinquents means that the process *can* be interrupted.

Longitudinal studies indicate that if the process is not interrupted, antisocial triad children end up experiencing a wide range of problems as adults. One such study was conducted by Glen Elder using data from families who experienced the Great Depression.(5) He followed the lives of two groups of children over a 30 year period. He found that children with a persistent pattern of temper tantrums seemed to go from one disaster to another through adolescence and into adulthood. They had stormy military and employment histories and were at greater risk for divorce and troubled marriages. They also tended to have irritable relationships with their own children! Thus, there not only seemed to be continuity and consequences for antisocial behavior throughout their own lifetime, but they were responsible for setting up the pattern to repeat itself in their children. Antisocial behavior can disrupt family life. It is not something that should be ignored, because it is very destructive.

The failure of antisocial children to develop good work skills and satisfying relationships with other people becomes more pronounced as they move from early into later adolescence. They talk back to teachers, and when this generalizes to talking back to employers, they find themselves losing one job after another. It is reasonable for antisocial adolescents and adults to make the assumption that other people don't like them, because it is true. But they tell themselves it doesn't matter because other people are stupid anyway, and so on. Such feedback loops seem to keep them locked into the process. They continue to deny responsibility for their failures, and the people around them become less tolerant. They find themselves generating increasingly complex explanations about why this cycle of failure is happening to them. Each failure locks them further into the cycle.

Interrupting the Process

This book is intended to help parents with adolescents prevent this process from occurring, or interrupt it if it has already started. Parents can change antisocial behavior patterns by following a step-by-step approach. In order to change the adolescent's behavior, however, the parent's behavior must change as well. Struggling with adolescents tends to make parents react with unpleasant responses of their own. This only makes things worse.

The first step in interrupting the antisocial process is to teach compliance at several different levels. This is the core behavior and changing it has a direct impact on the other two behaviors in the antisocial triad: temper tantrums, and avoiding responsibility. One of the reasons compliance is such an important issue is because the parent's behavior (making a request or giving an instruction) is directly tied to the adolescent's response. Parents can make the behavior happen by simply making a request. This means parents can choose the time and place for practice sessions in which they reinforce compliance, and remove privileges for noncompliance. The following section describes three basic levels of compliance.

Three Levels of Compliance Training

Sometimes compliance means the adolescent is expected to respond immediately to a request. Another level of compliance training is teaching children to be generally cooperative so they learn how to share with others and work as part of a team. Cooperation also means being willing to contribute to the household without being nagged. At other times compliance refers to how teenagers respond to house rules, and whether or not they have developed the self-control necessary to behave appropriately when their parents are not present. These are all part of what we mean when we talk about the overall level of compliance in adolescents. We will consider each in turn and describe how they relate to everyday family life, and then discuss the parents' role in teaching teenagers about them.

Immediate Compliance

Sometimes a parental request requires instant compliance, without question. For the toddler or young child these are typically situations in which physical injury is imminent, either to the child or others. (For example, "Don't touch the burner!" "Come out of the street!" "Stop hitting your brother." "Don't jump off the slide!!" "Stop throwing sand at your friends!")

Other requests that require an immediate response are less urgent, but they are important for maintaining peace and harmony in the family. (For example, "Stop arguing with me." "Quit picking on your little sister.") These requests are generally used to stop unpleasant behaviors.

Creative parents are able to turn many of these "stop" requests into "start-up" requests that initiate positive behaviors. (For example, "I can't see your point when you use that tone of voice. Write down the main points and then we'll discuss it." "Go to your room and get started on your homework now" [instead of teasing]). These requests are designed to engage the child in positive behaviors that are incompatible with continuing the problematic ones. Many parents are good at this type of redirection when their children are young, but seem to lose the skill when their children become teenagers. Start-up requests are better than stop requests because they are less likely to result in an argument.

Cooperation

Another level of compliance parents teach their children is how to cooperate with others. Cooperation means working together to achieve a common goal. This involves taking the needs and wishes of others into consideration, which requires moving away from self-interest. Before children can learn to be cooperative, however, they must be taught to be reasonably compliant. Cooperation can only take place in the absence of power struggles in which one person wins and the other person loses.

Cooperation requires a high level of compliance that is increasingly evident in children as they grow older. By the time your children reach adolescence, your job as a parent is to encourage them to voluntarily contribute to the household. At this point parents should be trying to move away from the need to use commands and requests to make their teenagers respond quickly. In other words, you should be helping them to develop the same awareness you have as an adult about the things that need to be done around the house. This dramatically reduces the need for nagging and issuing requests and commands. It also prepares them for life on their own. Parents won't always be around to tell their adolescents to do the dishes before they rot in the sink, or to pick up their clothes. As children grow older they need to take care of routine tasks without being asked. But you can't teach them how to be cooperative if you haven't taught them to comply with reasonable requests.

Creating a pleasant social atmosphere is an important part of developing a cooperative spirit in adolescents. Given that your adolescent is reasonably compliant, the next step in teaching cooperation is to foster good feelings among all members of the family. Good feelings come from having good times together. Make sure you do fun things as a group frequently so that you are not always working around the house, or solving problems. Caring for the needs and feelings of others means more than just helping to clean the house; it also means providing mutual support and sharing positive experiences.

Another important factor in teaching adolescents to cooperate is giving clear, friendly instructions. Good instructions, delivered in a pleasant manner, insure both compliance and cooperation. If adolescents know exactly what is expected of them, they are much more likely to do it. This is a win/win situation. The parents are happy because the adolescents are contributing to the family without being nagged, and the adolescents are happy because they don't feel pushed (the interaction is not perceived as a power struggle). The *way* you make your requests has a dramatic impact on whether or not your children respond cooperatively. All it takes is one negative or critical comment from parents to precipitate a power struggle. This is such an important point that the next chapter is devoted to describing how to make requests that work.

House Rules

By the time children enter grade school they are ready to learn about house rules. If you are constantly reminding your children about specific rules, it is time to write them down. House rules prescribe the expectations for specific behaviors and guidelines for living together as a group.

When children reach adolescence, it becomes increasingly important to have a set of well-defined house rules. Adolescents tend to "forget" certain important details such as the fact that they are supposed to be home for dinner at 6 o'clock. Writing down the house rules and posting them in a convenient place reduces the potential for arguments about whether a particular rule exists and how it is interpreted. Our list of house rules was attached to the inside of one of the kitchen cabinet doors.

Parents can use house rules to outline their expectations for specific behaviors. This usually involves setting limits. If, for example, your adolescent son develops a habit of staying out later than he should on school nights, then you need to establish a house rule which states, "The curfew on school nights is 10:30." Sometimes just writing down a specific rule will help solve the problem. But if the rule is violated more than once or twice, it may be necessary to add a consequence for breaking the rule. Some parents take away weekend car privileges for curfew violations on school nights, or change the curfew to 10:00 for a few days. The consequence should be applied every time house rules are broken even if the adolescent provides a convincing explanation about the reasons for doing it. The rules should be enforced consistently, otherwise you will be leaving yourself open to endless arguments about "exceptions to the rules." This makes it clear to the adolescent that the rules stand regardless of the circumstances.

Parents can also use house rules to spell out the standards of conduct for group living. This usually involves issues of privacy and respect. Some examples would be rules concerning speaking politely, knocking on closed doors before entering, and picking up personal belongings. Everyone in the household should agree to abide by these rules, otherwise the parents will end up mediating one dispute after another. If you find that certain "living problems" come up repeatedly, it is time to create a new house rule to prevent them from occurring.

As family members learn to follow house rules automatically, the rules on the cabinet door need to be changed. House rules should be tailored to deal with current problems. If putting the milk away after you are done with it is no longer a problem, the rule should be removed from the list. Then it is time to negotiate a new set of rules that are more appropriate to the age and sophistication of your child. The only house rules that need to be posted are the ones that are not being followed consistently. In our house, for example, one rule that was generally understood but not posted was, "The mess in your room is your own business, but don't let your stuff spill over into the general living area of the house or it will be confiscated." Whenever one of the adolescents forgot and left something lying around on the floor or countertops, it would disappear. The culprit could get it back, but he or she had to ask for it first, and the request was usually delivered with a sheepish expression. This reduced the clutter around the house and the nagging about putting things away.

Each family should establish its own set of five or ten house rules. Family members are more likely to cooperate if they help negotiate the house rules. (You may want to take a look at the chapters on communication and problem solving in Part 2 of this mini-series for guidelines on how to talk about these issues as a family.) Some of the house rules should reflect your wishes, and others should reflect the preferences of your children. The following is a list of some of the house rules that other families live by.

House Rules

1. Dinner will be ready at around 6 o'clock. and everyone is expected to be home and ready to eat at that time.

2. If you make a mess, you clean it up.
3. Family members are required to speak courteously to each other.
4. Going out on school nights must be negotiated in advance. All school work must be caught up.
5. Ask before borrowing things that belong to others. Borrowed items must be returned to their proper places in good condition. If you break something that belongs to someone else while you are using it, you are responsible for replacing it.
6. Parties must be prearranged, and an adult must be present during the party.
7. Knock and wait for a response before opening someone's closed door.
8. Only same sexed youngsters are allowed in the home without an adult present. No more than two at a time.
9. During weekdays, curfew is 10:30. On weekends, curfew is midnight.
10. If you borrow the car, it must be returned with the same amount of gas that it had when you borrowed it. Failure to do so will result in loss of car privileges.

Adhering to house rules represents a relatively high level of socialization. Children must be reasonably compliant and cooperative before you can expect them to consistently follow house rules. In many cases, parents with adolescents don't know whether the rules are being broken. For example, a rule about how many teenagers can be in the house while the parents are away is difficult for parents to monitor, although showing up "unexpectedly" every now and then will give you some idea about how well your adolescent is doing with a rule like this. But simply stating a rule is not enough. Parents must be willing to apply a consequence when the rules are violated. (Guidelines for using consequences are provided in Chapter 6.) Otherwise the rules will have little impact on the behavior of family members. Your first homework assignment is to come up with a set of house rules to help solve some of the problems that are occurring in your family.

Key Ideas in this Chapter

1. Compliance training begins early in the development of the child. This training is intimately related to the issue of socialization.
2. Noncompliant children tend to have severe adjustment problems.
3. The Antisocial Triad is made up of three behaviors: non-compliance, temper tantrums, and avoiding responsibility. Children who engage in these behaviors at high rates are at risk for adjustment problems.
4. There are many unpleasant consequences for the people who are in contact with Antisocial Triad children.
5. The process by which Antisocial Triad children develop severe adjustment problems can be interrupted.
6. There are three levels of compliance training: immediate compliance, cooperation, and following house rules.

Chapter One Homework Assignment: House Rules

You probably have some house rules already in effect in your family. Think about the rules that your children follow consistently, and write them down. These can be used to compliment your children for current successes.

The next step is to think of several behaviors or living situations that require constant reminding. Write these down as well, but don't share them with your children yet. First, tell them about the purpose of house rules, and ask them to write down two or three rules that would make *them* happier as members of the family. Encourage them to write down what they *want* rather than what they don't like. For example, "I want people to write telephone messages down immediately and put them on the refrigerator," rather than, "I *never* get my telephone messages." It is important for both parents and children to be specific and friendly in their requests. Have everyone write each request or rule on a separate piece of paper and put them into a suggestion box. Announce that the box will be opened on a specific date and the ideas will be discussed one at a time (allow two or three days for family members to collect ideas).

When you open the box, make sure everyone is there. Spend a few minutes considering each idea as a family. The point is to establish whether or not the ideas will help things go more smoothly in the family. At the end of the discussion, the parents should select one rule and the children should select one rule. These should be written down and posted in a convenient location.

Everyone should be involved in tracking whether or not the rules are being followed. Each instance should be labeled verbally. If someone follows a rule, family members should make a positive comment. Violations should be calmly noted by saying something like, "Melissa was 30 minutes late coming home from school today." When parents have their own shortcomings pointed out, they should try to be receptive to the feedback. For example, "Dad forgot to knock on my door before coming into my room today," should be followed by a response such as, "Oh, I guess you're right! I'll try to be better about that in the future. I apologize for interrupting your privacy." Parents can show their children how to react positively to feedback such as this by providing good role models.

In subsequent homework assignments, consequences will be added for violating house rules. But for now, simply try to notice whether or not house rules are consistently followed and label what you see.

Chapter One References

1. Eibesfeldt, I. "Phylogenetic Adaptation as Determinants of Aggressive Behavior in Man." In J. DeWit and W. W. Hartup (Eds.), *Determinants and Origins of Aggressive Behavior*. The Hague, Paris: Mouton, 1974.

2. The studies on social skill deficits of antisocial children were reviewed in Chapter 2 in Patterson, G. R. *A Social Learning Approach*, Volume 3: *Coercive Family Process*. Eugene, OR: Castalia Publishing Company, 1982.

3. The studies on reduced responsiveness to noncontingent social reinforcers were reviewed in Chapter 5 in Patterson, G. R. *A Social Learning Approach*, Volume 3: *Coercive Family Process*. Eugene, OR: Castalia Publishing Company, 1982.

4. The concept of reciprocity (that is, "you get what you give") is defined and discussed in Chapter 9 in Patterson, G. R. *A Social Learning Approach*, Volume 3: *Coercive Family Process*. Eugene, OR: Castalia Publishing Company, 1982.

5. The most influential programmatic work on the topic of irritability is by Glen Elder and his colleagues at the University of North Carolina. The following chapter is recommended reading: Elder, G. H., Liker, J. K., and Cross, C. E. "Parent Child Behavior in the Great Depression: Life Course and Intergenerational Influences." In P. B. Baltes & O. G. Brim (Eds.), *Life Span Development and Behavior*, Vol. 6. New York: Academic Press, 1983.

CHAPTER 2

Using Requests that Work

In the first chapter we discussed how socialization is related to children learning to be reasonably compliant and learning new skills; we also discussed how this process is disrupted in families with antisocial triad children. In addition, it was pointed out that compliance training must take place at several different levels. The homework assignment was to establish some house rules and practice labeling whether or not family members follow them.

This chapter shows parents how to encourage compliance by paying attention to the requests they make of their children. In general, good requests are: 1) few in number; 2) delivered in a polite and pleasant manner; 3) statements rather than questions; 4) well timed; 5) able to stand by themselves; 6) specific; 7) start-up requests instead of stop requests; and 8) succinct.

Limiting Requests

Few parents are aware of the number of requests they

make. Most of us would estimate an average of five or six requests each day; yet when trained observers record family interactions in home settings, they find that the rate for normal mothers is over 17 requests per hour.(1) Mothers from problem families use requests at a rate of over 27 per hour!

The relationship between the rate of requests issued by parents and problem behavior in children was explored in two studies carried out at the University of Oregon.(2) In these experiments with normal families, parents were asked to make their children behave like problem children. To accomplish this, most of the parents simply increased the rate at which they made requests—this doubled the rate of problem behaviors (including noncompliance) in these children. The results of this study indicate that if parents make too many demands on their children, they make things worse. Instead of slowing down problem behaviors, it actually adds fuel to the fire. For this reason it is important to pay attention to how often you are asking your youngster to do something. If you do it too much, you simply create problems for yourself.

The high rate of commands and requests that characterizes parents with problem children is due to several factors. The less time parents spend teaching their children social skills and cooperation, the more time they have to spend telling them to *stop* problem behaviors. The catch-22 is that when parents increase their rate of requests, it accelerates problem behaviors. This creates a hopeless situation in which the parents and children become enmeshed in one conflict after another. Parents who are caught up in this process often fail to realize that it is not possible to change the problem behaviors with commands alone. They must deal with the basic issue of teaching their children to do what they are supposed to do without having to nag them about it. This long, slow process is accomplished by telling children what to do and what not to do, then reinforcing them when they comply and using mildly unpleasant consequences, such as removing privileges, when they don't. This training sets the stage for how easy or difficult it is to manage your children in general. The next several chapters will show you how to do this.

Teenagers are better socialized than young children because they have been exposed to the socialization process for a longer period of time. They generally don't require as much direct instruction, which is a good thing since most of them have a low tolerance for being told what to do. With adolescents each request is an opportunity for conflict; so it's best to limit them.

Make Requests Politely and Pleasantly

These two aspects of making requests are particularly important, but often forgotten by parents. If your children tend to respond irritably (that is, they are easily annoyed, testy, and overly sensitive to your requests), you have probably slipped into the habit of using sarcasm or an angry tone of voice as well. It is the feeling behind the request that counts—expressing your angry feelings almost guarantees an unpleasant response. Parents need to pay attention to how they deliver requests to their children. Ask your spouse or a good friend to listen to you, and provide some feedback about your style (but only if you can do this without getting into an argument). If you find that you are using a negative style in making requests, try pretending that you are asking a good friend to do something and be as polite and cheerful as possible. For some unfortunate reason, most of us habitually treat members of our own family with less respect than we give good friends or complete strangers. Even if you feel aggravated because the request pertains to something that should have been done automatically, such as putting dirty socks in the hamper, resist the temptation to use sarcasm or a hostile tone of voice. It is also important not to use "put

41

downs" or to mention past failures when you are making a request. It is easy to "lose your cool" when you are tired or upset, but if you do, you are setting the stage for a conflict, and that will be unpleasant for both of you.

Use Statements Rather than Questions

When you make requests, deliver them as statements rather than as questions. Asking your youngsters if they would like to do something that you *expect* them to do gives them the opportunity to legitimately say "no," which leads most parents into giving a lengthy lecture. If you want adolescents to do something, then don't offer them a choice. To illustrate the point, let's compare two approaches to making the same request:

Mom: Alice, how would you like to feed the cat?
Alice: No thanks, mom. I'm busy right now.
Mom: It's your job to feed the cat. Why do I always have to tell you to do it? Don't you ever think about anyone but yourself?

Let's try it again using a statement instead . . .

Mom: Alice, please feed the cat now. She hasn't eaten all day.
Alice: I can't, mom, I'm busy.
Mom: Alice, feed her *now*. (using a firm, but neutral tone of voice)

Timing Requests

The timing of requests is absolutely critical. If your timing is bad, your request is almost certain to be met with rebellion. Even when you have to remind your adolescent son to do something he should have taken care of earlier, it is not a good idea to remind him when he is watching his favorite television show, talking to his girlfriend on the telephone, or doing his homework. It is better to wait until a commercial comes on, he hangs up the telephone, or he takes a break from his homework. Then make the request pleasantly, even if it's something he should have done hours ago. It does no good to get angry about it. The best way to avoid an argument and make sure that the job gets done is to stay calm and state what you want done. If you must interrupt, write a note and use a pleasant or humorous tone. Slip it to him and turn away quickly so you won't have to see his response.

Make One Request at a Time

Many parents save up their requests for a couple of days, and then dump them on their children all at once. For example, "Janet, I want you to clean your room, vacuum the rug, get your stuff off the dining table and put it away, and then get started on your homework." This is sure to trigger non-compliance. Even if Janet is willing to try to satisfy this chain of requests, she's bound to forget one or two of them. The typical parent reaction to Janet's performance would be to emphasize what Janet didn't do, rather than responding to what she actually accomplished. For this reason, it is important to make only *one* request at a time. Using contracts that list the things to be done on a regular basis is one way to get around this problem (guidelines for using contracts are provided in Part 2 of this mini-series).

Be Specific

Make your requests so specific that a stranger would understand what you mean. In some families, it is assumed that everyone knows what is meant by the statement, "Be home at a reasonable hour." What is reasonable to you is seldom reasonable to a teenager. It is better to say, "Be home by midnight, Cinderella." This removes any possibility for misunderstanding the request. If you want something done by a certain time, state that as part of the request.

43

("Please remember to finish the dishes before you use the telephone.")

Use Start-Up Requests

As we have already mentioned, making start-up requests instead of stop requests is an effective diversionary tactic when adolescents are doing something that you don't want them to do. Instead of telling them to *stop* doing something (which usually results in an argument), it is better to tell them to *start* doing something else that will make it impossible for the problem behavior to continue.

Let's assume, for example, that you are sitting in the living room enjoying some well-deserved quiet time, when a "storm" begins to brew in one of the kids' rooms. You've told the children over and over again not to fight, and yet there they go again. Why can't they learn to cooperate?

Dad Stays Calm While Using a Start-up Request

All right you guys, knock it off! Jennifer, go do your homework—and Stuart, get started on the dishes.

44

At this point you could do one of several things, but most of them would be ineffective. Before taking action, think about what it is that you want—you want peace, and you want it right away. Yelling at them from your comfortable chair won't have the desired effect. Going into the room and trying to find out what is going on and who caused the problem won't do it either, even if you tell them assertively, but without being irritable, to stop fighting. If your family is like most, this will only start an argument, or inspire a creative explanation about who was at fault. A much better alternative is to separate the children and get them started on something productive. You could say, for example, "Erik, you go and get started on your homework in the family room, and Jane, you start cleaning up your bedroom right now." Don't let yourself be drawn into acting as a mediator for the argument. Simply tell them to start doing something else. This will not only end the dispute, but will engage the children in constructive activities. Finding out who was at fault is seldom useful, since both children probably contributed to the problem.

Streamline Requests

Many parents slip into the habit of smothering their requests in a flurry of words. Worst of all, their requests may be delivered in the form of a lecture. These parents like to think that providing a rationale (with a little guilt mixed in for good measure) increases the likelihood that the children will cooperate. Unfortunately, this technique actually tends to decrease compliance. Teenagers worth their salt ignore the request and go after flaws in the rationale. The request is then lost in the ensuing free-for-all. If compliance eventually follows, it is only after a lengthy argument. It is best to discuss the underlying rationale at another time. The rule of thumb here is to state the request succinctly, and make it specific.

Act I: Auntie Pasta Needs Help

In the following scene, a group of adults work together to elicit cooperation from two adolescent girls who hadn't thought of helping in the kitchen. It wasn't that the girls were being "bad" by not volunteering, they simply hadn't thought of it. As you read this scene, notice the various types of requests made by the adults and the responses they receive.

The scene takes place two days after Thanksgiving. A group of families is spending the four-day weekend together in a lodge in the mountains. There is a light dusting of snow covering the ground. It is evening, and everyone has had a good time skiing and listening to music together. It is Auntie P.'s turn to cook, and she is busy preparing a gourmet Italian dinner. A large pile of dishes is stacked on the counter beside the sink, and the kitchen is a mess. The energy level accelerates as Auntie P. enlists help from the other people who are milling around the kitchen. Company is joining the group for dinner, and Auntie wants everything to be perfect. To accomplish this, Auntie knows that the group will have to work together as a team.

Marlena and Jack own the lodge. Marie is Marlena's 16-year-old goddaughter. Lynda and Harry are the parents of the other 16-year-old girl, Aileen. Auntie P. is a single woman.

Auntie Pasta: (sighing heavily) This kitchen is a mess! How will I ever be able to get anything done here?

(Marlena is busily wiping counters, throwing out trash and stacking dirty dishes in the sink.)

Marlena: Jack, it would make it a lot easier to cook dinner if someone would do the dishes.

46

Jack:	I'd volunteer, but I washed the breakfast dishes this morning.
Marlena:	Well, I don't know where these came from, but the sink is full of dirty dishes.
Jack:	I don't know where they came from either.
Marlena:	(sighing and using a martyred tone of voice) Alright, I guess I'll have to wash them myself then.
Jack:	If you wanted me to do them, why didn't you ask?
Marlena:	I did.
Auntie Pasta:	(to Marlena) But Marlena, your request wasn't very direct, was it?

(Marlena offers no response. She leaves the room quietly and goes to the bathroom. When she returns, Jack is already at the kitchen sink. In a cheerful tone of voice he calls out to Marie. . .)

Jack:	Hey Marie, I think you and I are on kitchen duty. Would you give me a hand?
Marie:	What do you want me to do?
Jack:	You dry and I'll wash. (He hands her a clean dishtowel.)
Auntie Pasta:	Aileen, here, you take this Olivada and spread it on these rounds of toast. Then sprinkle the chopped tomatoes on top.

(Aileen carefully spreads the Olivada on the toast, but haphazardly heaps on the tomatoes.)

Auntie Pasta:	(with a warm smile and a pleasant tone of voice) No, Aileen, not that way. Just put four or five pieces of tomato on top, and put them on so it looks pretty. This is supposed to be a work of art.

Marie:	(still drying dishes, she walks over to Marlena and asks) Where do the pots go?
Marlena:	The pots all go under the counter, and put them in neatly please. Maybe you could arrange them for me—they're really a mess.
Marie:	(meaning to be humorous, but sounding sarcastic) If I didn't make the mess, I shouldn't have to clean it up, right?
Auntie Pasta:	(again with a warm smile and a pleasant tone) Straighten it up quickly because I need you to help me with this antipasto. Somewhere there's a can of anchovies. After you finish with the pans, please find it, open it up, and drain off the oil. Then put some around the platter. And remember, let's try to make it beautiful.
Aileen:	(in a slightly petulant tone of voice) I thought *I* was helping you.
Auntie Pasta:	But honey, you are! I need lots of help. There's a lot to be done here, and I need at least two helpers.
Marie:	So what do you want me to do? Clean out the pots and pans cabinet or do the anchovies thing?
Auntie Pasta:	I need you to help me with both.
	(A frown flashes across Marie's face, but she says nothing and begins working on the pots and pans. Meantime, Harry is sitting beside Lynda's bed checking on her state of health. She has been ill, perhaps with a touch of food poisoning. She has been vomiting violently all day long, and Harry is concerned about her.)
Auntie Pasta:	(to Aileen) Take this glass of wine to Harry.

Aileen:	Let him get it himself. He's not doing anything.
Auntie Pasta:	(in the same friendly, but firm tone of voice) He is too! He's comforting your mother. Now do as I say, and take him this glass of wine.
	(Aileen does it, but she rolls her eyes at Marie as she leaves the kitchen. The two girls snicker.)
Marlena:	(Marlena comes over to the cabinet where Marie is working and silently gives her a hand. When they are done she says. . .) Great, Marie! Thanks for doing such a good job. (Then she hands her the anchovies and the can opener, and without another word walks over and gives Jack a quick hug. He is still up to his elbows in dirty dishwater.)

In this scene, the adults did a good job of working together. As in any normal family situation, there were many opportunities for the exchanges between the teenagers and the grownups (and between the grownups as well) to deteriorate into unpleasant interactions; but each hostile or near-hostile comment was intercepted and diverted. As everyone knows, it is sometimes difficult to stay out of arguments. Let's go back over this scene to see just how this was done.

It is important to notice that everyone in this scene has just spent the day having fun together. Playing together makes it possible to break out of the negative sets that build up between family members (it makes deposits in the interpersonal "bank account").

It is also important to point out that in this situation everyone would benefit by helping out. When the preparations are completed, there will be a grand feast. It is also true that everyone contributed to the mess in the kitchen that needed to be cleaned up. Now it was time for everyone to cooperate and put things back in order so that dinner could be prepared.

In this scene, the first request was Auntie's. It was easy to overlook because it was made indirectly, "This kitchen is a mess." Marlena was already helping, so her response was to follow Auntie's request with one of her own, "Jack, it would make it a lot easier. . ." The first noncompliant response was Jack's, ". . . but I washed the dishes this morning." This response could easily have provoked an argument, but it was skillfully deflected by Auntie's quick response, and by Marlena leaving the scene. Jack took the hint, and began washing the dishes without getting angry about it.

Notice the way Jack requested Marie's assistance. If he had given her a direct order such as, "Marie, get in here and help. You haven't done anything all weekend," and delivered the message with a touch of hostility in his voice, she probably would have responded with a negative comment of her own instead of complying with the request.

When Auntie wanted to enlist the help of Aileen, she started by giving her some general instructions "Spread the olivada and sprinkle tomatoes. . ." Then she gave Aileen some corrective feedback, but it was done in a positive, or at least neutral, way. Again, this kept the situation from turning into an argument.

The next request sequence was directed at putting the pots and pans away. Auntie helped to deflect Marie's comment to Marlena by asking her to do something that was more fun than putting the pots in the cabinet, that is, help with the antipasto, which immediately drew a complaint from Aileen. Auntie P. was also able to deflect this comment by making a general statement that she needed lots of help. What she meant was that this was not the time to quibble about who does what—it was time for everyone to get their jobs done so that the dinner could be prepared.

When Aileen was asked to do something nice for her stepfather, she automatically refused; once again Auntie deftly changed the situation by telling Aileen that he was helping out by taking care of Lynda, who was sick. Aileen then complied with the original request, although she expressed her discontent by rolling her eyes at Marie. This low level act of insolence was appropriately ignored by all.

Meanwhile, Marie was getting bogged down with her task of arranging the pots and pans. This situation was defused by her godmother, who matter-of-factly helped her finish the project, thanked her for doing a good job (thus rewarding her for complying with the request), and silently urged her on to the next task by handing her the can of anchovies.

Thus, the day was saved and the dinner was prepared in record time. Everyone had a chance to sit and talk before the company came and dinner was served. A good time was had by all.

Your first homework assignment for this chapter is to track how you make requests and to try using the guidelines presented here for using requests that work. This is very important, because whether or not your children comply with your requests is determined in part by how they are delivered.

Working on Noncompliance

Parents come to see us at the Oregon Social Learning Center because they need help in managing their adolescent and preadolescent children. It is not surprising that most of these parents identify noncompliance as the basic problem. There is a very straightforward way to determine whether or not your adolescents are reasonably compliant. Simply make a request, and see if they comply. This is the second part of your homework assignment (the details are provided at the end of this chapter). If adolescents don't comply with routine requests at home, then they probably aren't complying with requests made by other people either. A low rate of compliance would strongly suggest that your adolescent is breaking many of your household rules as well.

In one of our own unpublished studies we observed a sample of 100 families with nonproblem 10- and 11-year-old boys to see how these boys responded to requests, demands, and threats made by other family members. They were observed for three sessions. The average rate of compliance to requests and demands made by mothers was 57%; there were only three boys in the entire sample who obeyed their mothers every time. Fathers didn't fare as well—the average rate of compliance to their requests was 47%. The study also confirmed what most parents already know about children honoring the requests of their siblings; the average rate of compliance to sibling requests was only 16%!

The results of these studies show it is not reasonable to expect your adolescent to comply with all of the requests you make as a parent; but a compliance rate of 50%–60% would indicate that your child falls within reasonable bounds. If this is not the case, then this is something you will need to work on. As we noted earlier in the chapter, improving the way in which you make requests is the first step.

In order to work on noncompliance parents need to be very clear about the definition of compliance and noncompliance. The therapists at Oregon Social Learning Center have talked to hundreds of parents about this set of behaviors. Almost everyone seems to agree that compliance means doing as asked within 10 to 15 seconds of the request. Does that seem unreasonable? Not if you use good timing and follow the other guidelines for making requests provided in this chapter. If you want something done *now* are you willing to wait two or three minutes for the response? Usually this only makes parents become angry because they have to think about the situation that much longer. This is also bad training for the adolescent who must learn to respond to requests by teachers and other adults in a timely fashion. When the teacher asks everyone to turn to page 17, it means *now*. For these reasons it is best to require an immediate response to your requests. This means that teenagers should be expected to carry out requests *the first time you tell them*.

Once you have defined compliance in this way, it is easy to come up with a definition of noncompliance. Very simply, noncompliance is not getting started within 10 or 15 seconds. Parents often want to count complaining about the request as noncompliance even if the adolescent carries out the request within the time specified. We think it is best for parents to ignore this behavior at first—otherwise you can easily become sidetracked. After you have some success at improving compliance, you can require your children to stop complaining when they are complying with your requests. Your chances of success are much better if you focus on one problem at a time.

Key Ideas in this Chapter

1. The way in which parents make requests is directly related to compliance/noncompliance in children.
2. We have discussed the importance of limiting requests, being polite, using statements rather than questions, having good timing, making one request at a time, being specific, using start-up requests, and streamlining your requests.
3. Compliance means getting started on carrying out the request within 15 seconds; any other response is defined as noncompliance.

Chapter Two Homework Assignment

Part One—Using Requests that Work

For the next two days, keep track of your requests. Pick a one-hour period when you and your adolescent are together and count every request you make. Use this chart to write down the results.

Parent Requests Chart

Quality of Requests	Day 1	Day 2
Good Requests	Total _____	Total _____
Bad Requests	Total _____	Total _____

Every time you follow the guidelines for good requests (well-timed, specific, pleasant, and so on) give yourself a mark in the "good requests" box. When you slip up, put a mark in the "bad requests" box. Record each request right away so you don't forget to write it down. If you find that using a pencil and paper to do this is awkward, you might consider using a golf counter that is worn on the wrist. This device looks like a watch, and has several counters on it that can be used to record good and bad requests.

If you are honest about recording your requests, you will have at least one or two marks in the "bad requests" box. Some parents may have quite a few. You will probably find that there are several areas you need to work on.

There are several ways to improve your skills. One is to use a tape recorder so you can listen to yourself making requests. Imagine one of the situations where you used a "bad request" and practice doing it correctly. Play the tape back so you can hear how you sound. Refine your presentation until it sounds like a "good request." You might want to enlist some help from a friend who can listen to you and provide some constructive feedback. One more trick is to count silently to 10 before you make requests. Use this time to practice making the request in your mind, imagine that your child is an adult, and *then* make the request.

Before moving on to the homework assignment for Part Two, you need to make sure that you are making "good requests" at least 50% of the time. You must also limit the number of requests you are making to avoid fueling noncompliance. Otherwise you defeat yourself.

Part Two—Tracking Compliance

Now your job is a little more difficult because you will be paying attention to your own requests *and* the way in which your adolescent responds to them. If you make a request, your child's response is either compliance or noncompliance.

Tell your teenager that you are starting to keep track of how often *you* make requests, and whether or not those requests are carried out. The following is a sample of the dialogue you might use to introduce this idea.

Some Changes Are Forthcoming

Dad: Kelly, in the next few weeks I'm going to be making some changes. Sometimes when I ask you to do things like take out the garbage or help around the house, we get into arguments and nothing happens. I think we can do better than that, so I'm going to start paying attention to what's going on between us. For one thing, I think *I* could be more polite when I ask you to help out and that might make things better. At any rate, I'm going to keep track of my requests and the way you respond to them.

Kelly: What do you mean, the way I respond?

Dad: I want to find out if you routinely do what I ask, or if you are in the habit of arguing with me about it.

Kelly: I *always* do what you tell me, eventually.

Dad: I suppose so, but I want you to do it without all the arguing we go through. I want us to get along better. And I'm going to try to pay attention to my own behavior as well.

Kelly: Do you think it will do any good?

Dad: Well, I'm not really sure, but I'm going to give it a try. This chart goes up on the refrigerator, and every time I ask you to do something like hang up your coat or shut the door, feed the cat, something like that, I'm going to rate myself for whether or not I was polite, and I'm going to rate you for whether or not you did as I asked.

Kelly: Does that mean I don't have to do something if you shout at me?

Dad: No, it just means I'm going to be paying attention to the fact that sometimes I shout and sometimes you don't mind. By the way, when I make a request, I expect you to get started right away—within 10 or 15 seconds. Then I won't have to keep nagging you about it.

Kelly: That's ridiculous!

Dad: Maybe so, but that's how it's going to be from now on. I promise to be careful about the timing of my requests, but it may not always be convenient for you.

Kelly: Well, that's great. Now I'm supposed to be some kind of robot that's completely under your control.

Dad walks calmly out of the room, even though he can think of several comments he would like to add. He has introduced the idea to his son, and that was the main purpose of the conversation. He knows it would be almost impossible to make Kelly gladly accept the change.

In part two of your homework assignment you will continue to pay attention to your requests, but now you will need to track the response of your adolescent by making a mark in the compliance/noncompliance boxes on the chart that follows. Try to develop an ear to hear yourself from the perspective of an uninvolved stranger so you can rate your request as good or bad. Then wait 15 seconds to see if your teenager responds by getting started. Write down these events right away. If you try to write them down later, you will distort the way things really happened. Try to be objective, even though it is difficult.

If you have to make the same request several times, put a mark in the noncompliance box each time this occurs. Notice whether your requests are becoming increasingly negative. Record each instance right away. It helps if you keep your chart in a handy place like the refrigerator door.

Requests/Compliance Chart

Parent Requests	Day ____	Day ____	Day ____	Day ____
Good Requests				
Bad Requests				
Adolescent Responses				
Compliance				
Noncompliance				

Requests/Compliance Chart

Parent Requests	Day _____	Day _____	Day _____	Day _____
Good Requests				
Bad Requests				
Adolescent Responses				
Compliance				
Noncompliance				

Chapter Two References

1. Patterson, G. R. *A Social Learning Approach*, Volume 3: *Coercive Family Process*. Eugene, OR: Castalia Publishing Company, 1982. The data relating to the rate of requests for mothers in normal and distressed families is presented in Table 12.1, page 276 (the code category for requests is "Command").

2. Lobitz, W. C., and Johnson, S. M. "Parental Manipulation of the Behavior of Normal and Deviant Children." *Child Development*, 1975, 46, 719-726.

See Also

Lobitz, G. K., and Johnson, S. M. "Normal versus Deviant Children: A Multi Method Comparison." *Journal of Abnormal Child Psychology*, 1976, 3(4), 353-373.

CHAPTER 3

Monitoring and Tracking—The Basics for Involved Parents

Monitoring and tracking are critically important skills for parents raising adolescents—they are the base upon which other parenting skills are constructed. Both terms refer to something that most parents do without much thinking.

Monitoring refers to how well parents keep track of their adolescents' behavior away from home. In order to be effective as parents, it is necessary to know the answers to the FOUR BASIC QUESTIONS: Who, Where, What, and When? Who are your adolescents with? Where are they? What are they doing? and When will they be home? Research has shown that parents who cannot provide adequate answers to these questions tend to have adolescents who are at risk for drifting into deviant peer groups, engaging in substance abuse, and delinquency.(1)

Tracking means focusing on the *details* of adolescent behavior. If you want to change things in your family, you must start by being specific about the behavior to be changed, and then keep track of how often the behavior occurs. If you completed the homework assignment in the previous chapter, you already have some experience in tracking parental requests and adolescent noncompliance. *Most of us do not track the behavior of the people around us very carefully, even if we care deeply about them.* We tend, instead, to form stereotypes that characterize their behavior. For example, we frequently use terms such as "lazy vs. ambitious," "uptight vs. relaxed," and "quiet vs. wild" when we are describing people. These are handy labels that describe the general style of a person's behavior. The problem with global statements such as these is they make it almost impossible to notice that somebody is *changing*. To notice small changes in behavior you have to break through these stereotypes. One of the best ways to do that is to track or pay careful attention to specific behaviors.

Monitoring: Seeing the Big Picture

Our studies suggest that prior to leaving high school most adolescents require a great deal of old-fashioned supervision in some crucial areas such as household duties, homework, and extracurricular activities.(2) Supervising your adolescent in these important areas is an act of love. The emphasis on permissive childrearing in the 1950s was a much needed antidote for centuries of extremely authoritarian and punitive childrearing practices. But our clinical and empirical studies strongly suggest that being too permissive can also cause problems. In order to be effective caregivers, parents need to be involved in their children's lives. Being aware of the big picture is part of this essential involvement.

Too much freedom can be a greater problem than too little freedom. Before adolescents are allowed to try out activities demanding high levels of self-control and good judgment, they must first prove that they can handle certain basics. Adolescents should *earn their freedoms one step at a time*. It takes practice to manage freedom, and parents need to monitor their children's progress during this learning process. It is also the parents' job to decide when their children are ready for the next step, and what each step will be. For example, before adolescents can be trusted to take care of the house for the weekend while their parents are away, they have to demonstrate that they can be left at home alone for shorter periods of time without breaking house rules. The first time they are left alone it should be for one night only, perhaps during the week, and it is probably a good idea to have someone stop by to check on them. If all goes well, try one weekend night, then two, and so on. Gradually, with each success, you can slow down the monitoring. But, during the early phases of "learning and earning," adolescents need to be carefully monitored by their parents. If they show that they can handle increasing degrees of freedom, then you can allow them to have more. If they abuse their freedom, then they should have less.

This is so obvious that you may wonder why it is necessary to bring it up at all. There are, however, many reasons why parents fail to supervise the behavior and activities of their adolescents. It takes time, energy, and commitment to do a good job of monitoring. Our recent studies suggest that parents with major stressors impinging on them (such as unemployment, illness, marital conflict, or divorce), and minor daily hassles (such as financial difficulties, household maintenance, and car problems) have a hard time monitoring their adolescents.(3) Parents who are heavy users of drugs or alcohol also have difficulty monitoring their children. Some parents just don't realize how important it is to provide close supervision for their teenagers. Other parents tell us they *can't* control their adolescents so they try to ignore the awful things they do, who they hang out with, or where they go when they are out on the town with their friends. A few parents have reported that they thought they were old-fashioned for being concerned about these things.

When both parents work, or a single parent works, it is more difficult to monitor children, but it still can be done effectively. If, for example, it has been agreed that the adolescent is supposed to be home by four o'clock, then the parent should make a telephone call from work at that time. Parents who can't call need to arrange for someone else to check in on their adolescents. Another alternative would be to arrange for the teenager to participate in some after-school activities that are supervised by adults.

Another aspect of monitoring involves spending pleasant time with your children. That means arranging your schedule so you can be around when your children are home. If you make this a priority, something can usually be worked out. Children who are consistently left alone at home during the evening hours have a hard time resisting the many temptations available to them. They need to have a caring parent around who is paying attention to what they are doing. Parents who are out of touch with their children's activities cannot provide guidance and corrective feedback.

Spending some good, focused time with your children is a great way to build a positive relationship with them. The relaxed conversations that take place between parents and their children on a day-to-day basis are important. They provide an opportunity for parents to learn about events in the lives of their adolescents. Your teenager may, for example, have given a speech in class and felt nervous about it. This is a good time to "tie into" the event by recounting how you felt in similar situations. This sharing of events brings parents closer to their children, and allows them to monitor what is going on in a relatively unobtrusive way. It is a chance for the adolescents to talk while their parents *actively listen*. What classes do they like, and which ones are difficult for them? How are things going with their friends?

These exchanges are genuine expressions of the fact that you care about your children. If you are an interested and understanding listener, you'll enjoy the friendly conversations you have with your adolescent. If, however, you use these conversations as an opportunity to pry information out of your children, and then proceed to deliver a lecture, or criticize their shortcomings, you will learn very little from them. If you do this often enough, you may end up joining the group of parents who say "My adolescent never talks to me." As you listen to their trials and tribulations as well as their pleasures and successes, try to visualize what they have experienced, and how it felt to them. Stop thinking about your own concerns, focus your attention on them, and try to understand what their world must be like. All it takes is 15 minutes each day of your undivided attention to make meaningful contact with your adolescent.

A very important part of monitoring is to maintain clearly defined rules about "street time." Street time means spending time with friends without the presence of teachers, parents, or other responsible adults. It is a good idea to write down the rules about street time because people tend to distort what they remember about these delicate issues. The rules should specifically address the following questions: When are they supposed to be home after school? What time are they expected to be home on weekends? What are the rules for going out on school nights? How many nights a week can they be out? Where are they going? Who are they with? What are they doing?

Studies show that children who are allowed to have a *great deal of unsupervised* street time are seriously at risk for drifting into the influence of a deviant peer group.(4) Extensive contact with the wrong peer group can contribute to a variety of problems ranging from drug and alcohol abuse to juvenile delinquency. Children involved in these activities tend to spend a great deal of time with peers who are engaged in similar activities. In this way, inadequate parental supervision is associated with being in deviant peer groups, which, in turn, may lead to drug and alcohol abuse and other delinquent activities. During the last 10 years, researchers have repeatedly demonstrated the connection between lack of adult supervision and deviant behavior in children. The consistency of these findings suggests that it is worthwhile for parents to know about this connection.

This has many implications for parents. For one thing, it means that it is important for you to meet your adolescent's friends. Try to keep in mind that even in the best of peer groups, there will be times when your youngsters are trying things out that they are not ready to handle. It is also true that all adolescents, no matter how good they are, make mistakes. That's why they all require some monitoring, especially when they are trying out new experiences. Parents can only provide some of the experiences that help adolescents learn to be adults. The other half of what they must learn at this stage is provided by their peers. It's up to you to try to prepare them for these new experiences so they will make the right decisions in your absence and, for example, turn down the dare to play chicken in a car, or have the self-control to say "no" when someone offers to turn them on to drugs. In this context, it is reassuring to note that national survey studies have shown that there is a reasonably good fit between what children learn from their peer group and what they have learned from their parents.(5) Only a *small* fraction of the adolescent population consistently has problems when they try out new experiences. Unfortunately, the media portray this tiny group of teenagers as though they represent all teenagers who test the rules. This is simply not the case—all teenagers test the rules to various degrees, but only a small group of them takes it to extremes.

Street time is a central issue that can become very complicated to negotiate. It is directly related to how much control parents have in supervising the behavior of their adolescents. Parents have the right and the responsibility to establish and enforce rules about street time. These rules provide a formal statement of what is acceptable and what is not. Some guidelines for setting up house rules were provided in Chapter 1: Teaching Compliance and The Readiness to be Socialized. In the homework assignment for that chapter you were instructed to create a list of house rules. You should make sure that you add some rules about street time to the list you already have. If you are unsure what is reasonable, ask other parents with teenagers the same age for some suggestions.

Act I: Paula Gets Her Way

The Scene. The following exchange takes place between the mother in a single-parent family, and her 14-year-old daughter. It's a week night and Paula, the daughter, has just appeared in the living room all dressed up. She's waiting to be picked up by her friends when her mother confronts her.

Mother: That's a great get up, what's going on tonight?
Paula: My friends are picking me up.
Mother: Which friends, and how come you're planning to go out on a school night? I think we need to talk about this.
Paula: (whirling around) What is this—some sort of interrogation or what? I've got a right to go out with my friends without being grilled by you.
Mother: You are not allowed to go out on school nights without talking to me first. You know that! I have to know where you're going, and who you're going out with. I also want to meet your friends.
Paula: Oh, NO! They would think that's weird. Be-

sides, they're here right now. I've gotta go—I don't have to put up with these police tactics. (She slams the door and rushes out to meet her friends in the car outside.)

In this scene Paula was in charge; she did exactly what she wanted to do. When the mother tried to establish some control, Paula had a mini-tantrum. If Paula continues to win by verbally attacking her mother, and running off when her mother tries to monitor her, the mother will eventually stop trying. Paula's mini-temper tantrum worked—she got her night out. The next time the mother tries to monitor her, she is very likely to repeat the tantrum. Paula is training her mother not to monitor her by punishing her when she does.

Paula's basic assumption is that her mother does not have the right to set limits or to bring up the topic of house rules. This also means that it would be very difficult for her mother to enforce the rules, since the adolescent did not agree to abide by them in the first place. The mother has to learn some new strategies so that she "wins" when Paula confronts her like this. That's what this book is about— teaching parents how to handle adolescents when they get out of control. The next several chapters outline how this is done.

In a study of several hundred families, the parents of fourth grade children said they allowed an average of about 45 minutes of unsupervised street time each week; for seventh graders it was one hour, and for tenth graders two hours.(6) These results indicate that as children grow older, most parents allow them to have more freedom. It is usually best to try out small increases in street time. When adolescents prove they are responsible about coming home on time, then gradually permit them to come home a little later in the evening. You may also want to check with other parents who have well-behaved adolescents to find out what curfews they have established.

It is important to remember that children do not have any God-given rights when it comes to privileges like driving the car (even if it's their own car), or spending unsupervised time with friends. If, for example, your adolescent son has just earned the right to take the car out by himself with friends, and you find out they were drinking or smoking pot, then a consequence should be applied (see Chapter 6 on discipline for more details). One logical consequence would be to remove all driving privileges for a month or two while your son repeats the earlier steps in the process of teaching him to be responsible when he uses the car. In this way the adolescent is required to earn back the privilege of driving the car. He will think twice about drinking or smoking when he is driving in the future.

It is up to the parents to make decisions about the kinds of experiences and activities their teenagers are ready to handle. These decisions should be based on what parents have observed about their teenager's past performances. This helps to insure that the adolescent will have a good experience with new freedoms. By the way, it is probably not reasonable to expect a perfect performance (as long as the transgressions are not frequent or of a serious nature). The process of letting go requires careful supervision. If the adolescent is doing well in handling new freedoms, the parents do not have to be as vigilant. By the time your adolescent is ready to leave home, very little monitoring will be necessary. But make sure that your teenager earns this adult status one small step at a time.

Tracking: Learning to Notice the Little Things

This section describes another type of monitoring. Instead of being concerned about seeing the big picture, tracking has to do with being aware of the small details that can easily slip by unnoticed. This molecular tracking is very important because it is a prerequisite for changing behavior. The discussion will begin by focusing on how people form stereotypes that describe the behavior of others, and what this does to the tracking process. After this, some techniques for tracking the details of adolescent behavior will be presented.

Breaking Down Stereotypes: When the Big Picture Is Too Big

Before you can change behavior, you must deal with the problem of breaking down stereotypes. The generalizations that we make about ourselves and others have a dramatic impact on the way that we perceive the events going on around us. You can't help your family change until you break free of your stereotypes.

Modern cognitive psychology tells us that creating stereotypes is part of the human condition.(7) We seem to build them as a cognitive survival technique. As human beings we have limited awareness.(8) That means our minds can only handle a small amount of information at any one moment. This forces you to pay attention to a few selected things, and to generalize your understanding of the events taking place by using stereotypes to fill in the gaps. Let's suppose, for example, that you are talking to a male acquaintance who tends to be sarcastic. After you have finished talking to him it is unlikely that you remember all of what he said, but you are very likely to remember the comments that were particularly caustic. These comments would then be incorporated into the stereotype you have constructed about this person and would strengthen your conviction that he is generally sarcastic. It would take many exchanges in which this person was pleasant before you would change your stereotype about him. Information that does not fit the stereotype is usually discounted, whereas information that fits the stereotype is readily incorporated.

70

Most of the time we are not tracking what is going on around us very carefully. It is impossible to notice and remember all of the details that are embedded in social interactions, such as what people are doing, their exact words, their facial expressions, and our reactions to them. What we do instead is to construct a generalized description that covers the highlights of each exchange, and let it go at that. This means there are huge holes in our understanding of ourselves and others, but we fill them in with stories that fit our stereotypes. Much of the extraordinary complexity in social interactions is handled in this way. This is one of the ways that our biological computers compensate for the fact that we can only pay attention to a few things at once.

After we meet someone new, for example, we tend to come away with a global impression of that person such as, "She seemed friendly," or "He looked awfully uptight." These are convenient labels that are easy to remember and they also give us an idea of what to expect when we meet that person again. These labels give us a feeling for whether we should avoid these people or seek them out.

Another way our biological computer helps us to deal with the complexity of social interactions is the tendency to develop habitual patterns of behaving. This allows us to operate on "automatic pilot" much of the time. We can do one thing while our attention is actually focused on something else. There is very little thinking necessary, for example, when you greet someone. Your initial statement is something like, "Hello, how are you?" The other person's response is typically something like, "Fine, and you?" and so on. These routine exchanges, and others like them, tend to run off in chains where the links are well established and require very little thought. The same thing is true for family interactions. Most of them are like the "How was your day?" exchanges. While these may be meaningful exchanges, they are run off without a lot of conscious effort because they follow a well-established format. The implication is that family members often react to one another without thinking very carefully about it. Acting without thinking is fine as long as you are doing something routine, or something that doesn't require your best effort. One example of this is driving a car. Experienced drivers can carry on a good conversation when driving conditions are straightforward; but when they are in a blizzard they need to focus all of their attention on driving the car, no matter how good their skills are. If you want to work on improving relationships in your family, you have to break out of automatic pilot and pay attention to what is actually going on.

Creating stereotypes and developing habitual patterns of responding to others can create problems. When we watch our children interacting with other family members, we listen to what they say, we notice their behavior, and then we fit it into the stereotypes we have constructed about them. This makes it difficult to recognize when people are changing. Once we have established stereotypes that we think describe people reasonably well, we expect them to stay that way forever. We pay attention to the things they say and do that fit our expectations, and we ignore the rest. For people we like or who are currently in our good graces, we tend to view their behavior in a positive light. If we're angry at them, no matter what they do to the contrary, we consider their actions and the consequences of those actions in a negative light.

It is important to realize that some of the stereotypes we have about people have *very little* to do with what is actually going on. For example, when we are depressed, many of our experiences seem to be dark and gloomy—even the good things seem lifeless and unenjoyable. Studies have consistently shown that depressed parents (most of the subjects were mothers) tend to *perceive* their children as deviant, even when home observations and reports by teachers and peers about the children do not support the mothers' descriptions.(9) These other sources of information suggested that only a very small number of the children showed evidence of behavior problems. For these mothers, depression was like a filter that selectively tuned in and intensified a negative view of the world.(10) Depression also changed the stereotypes these women had about themselves and other family members: "I am a bad person, with a terrible future, living in a world of bad people. My children are bad people too." Part of the problem in working with such parents is to get them to shift their stereotypes about family members and themselves. Teaching these mothers how to carefully track *specific* behaviors was one of the techniques we developed at our research center to help them break out of this bleak world view. Interestingly enough, when they learned to become more effective as parents, they also began to feel better about themselves, and their depression significantly decreased.(11)

The question is, once you have established stereotypes about someone, how can you change them? In the preceding example it was mentioned that tracking helps, but how does paying attention to the details of someone's behavior break down these stereotypes? A classic study by R. Wahler initiated a whole series of studies on this topic.(12) Dr. Wahler showed videotapes of an extremely out-of-control young boy to a group of adults. After viewing the videotapes, each adult was asked to rate how hyperactive the boy was. Since none of the adults in the study had ever met the boy before, these ratings represented the stereotypes the adults had created about the boy. Half of the adults were then trained to pay attention to specific aspects of the boy's behavior. They learned to track how many times the boy disrupted the classroom, how many times he got out of his seat, and how often he completed his homework assignments. They tracked his behavior by observing and recording these events as they watched several more hours of videotapes. The other half of the adults simply watched the same videotapes without counting specific behaviors. Then Dr. Wahler did an extremely interesting thing. He had both groups of adults look at a new set of videotapes where the boy's behavior improved steadily until he became better than the average child.

It took a while for the adults who were trained to track the boy's behavior to notice the improvement and change their initial stereotypes. Eventually they could see that the boy had improved a great deal. The adults in the untrained group, however, held on to their stereotypes. Even when the boy's behavior was in the normal range, they failed to notice any significant improvement.

It is hard to change the stereotypes you have developed about the people around you, but it can be done *if you pay attention to smaller, more specific behaviors.* What this does is to help you view the world with "new eyes," that is, to look at your own family the way that a baby or stranger would. This is the first step toward making significant changes in the way family members relate to one another. Although it may seem as if you are accomplishing very little by merely tracking the details of your adolescent's behavior, this is the foundation for the rest of the techniques outlined in this book.

Methods for Tracking Behavior

People in the first blush of romance generate positive stereotypes of each other. This is one of the reasons they are unable to see important flaws in each other. People in conflict, on the other hand, generate negative stereotypes about each other. If you and your adolescent are not getting along, both of you are probably making up angry stories about the other person that have little to do with what is actually going on. You might be surprised to hear the stories your teenager tells about you. It is also very likely that you are exaggerating the negative aspects of your adolescent's behavior. You may have thoughts like, "That lazy kid—he only thinks of himself!" But there are three things wrong with this description of your child.

1. It is too general.
2. It doesn't describe the specific behaviors needing to be *decreased*.
3. It doesn't describe the good behaviors needing to be *increased*.

To illustrate these points, let's say your 13-year-old boy acts like he is a house guest. When he comes in the door

The 13-Year-Old House Guest

Hey Mom—hurry up with dinner so I can play basketball with the guys...

after school, it's like the dance of the seven veils—his scarf is draped on the hallway chair, his jacket is thrown on the couch, and his books are heaped on the kitchen counter on the way to the refrigerator. He makes a snack and doesn't put the food away. For his marathon shower, he uses *all* of the hot water. And, to top it all off, you have a hard time getting him to do chores. Even though this list of behaviors is incomplete, it is a good first step toward being specific about what was implied in the global statements "lazy" and "thinks only of himself."

Most behaviors have two sides, the PROBLEM and its REPLACEMENT. Instead of thinking only about himself, *what is it that you want him to DO?* If your response is "To think of people other than himself," that is in the right spirit, but you must be more specific. If you can't see specific behaviors, you cannot see tiny changes over time and you won't be able to respond to them contingently. This leads us to consider the following rules for selecting and tracking behaviors:

1. Be specific about the problem behavior and its replacement. Most of the behaviors that concern you as a parent are somewhat ambiguous, but it is necessary for you to spell them out in detail. If your description of both the problem behavior and its replacement are clear enough that a stranger could tell when they are occurring, then you have a good definition. This is not as difficult as it sounds. Most problem behaviors have an opposite. If you can be specific about one, then the other more or less suggests itself. Let's say that the thing that bothers you the most about your teen-age daughter is her "bad attitude" and you have decided to track and try to change this behavior. The term "bad attitude" is really too global for a stranger to know what you mean. How can you come up with a definition that is more specific?

Begin by looking for examples of good and bad attitude

for a couple of days. For example, at dinner last night you may have seen an outstanding sample of bad attitude when your daughter was talking back, swearing, interrupting, and arguing. Later that evening, when she wanted to borrow the car, you may have seen an example of "good attitude." During this exchange she spoke to you politely, in a pleasant tone of voice, with a smile on her face. Then, after you told her she couldn't use the car, you saw another example of "bad attitude" when she started yelling and throwing things. For a grand finale she stormed into her room and slammed the door. Now the definition of your daughter's attitude is becoming specific enough for a stranger to be able to count positive and negative instances of it. Good attitude includes: being polite, smiling, and talking in a pleasant tone of voice. For bad attitude, you also have a list of several behaviors: talking back, swearing, interrupting, arguing, throwing things around, yelling, and slamming doors. Over a period of days you would be able to come up with a list of behaviors that describes in detail what you mean by good and bad attitude, a list so specific that any English-speaking person would be able to look at your definitions and start counting.

2. Start with problems you can see. We realize that many of the important problems that concern parents with adolescents take place when the youngsters are away from home. These problems include truancy, shoplifting, drug and alcohol use, cigarette smoking, sexual behavior, and racing around in cars. There are extra steps involved in monitoring adolescents when they are away from home. At this beginning stage, it is better to select target behaviors you can see.

Here are some examples of behaviors that are usually easy to "see": doing homework (either studying at home when you are there or showing you the completed work), being on time, doing chores, compliance, returning the car in good condition (no dings, proper amount of gas, clean, on time, proper place in yard or garage, etc.), and getting along with siblings when you are around.

3. Start with relatively neutral behaviors. When you start negotiating with your adolescent about the changes that need to be made, it is much easier if you begin by dealing with problem behaviors that do not infuriate you. If you are irritated when you are trying to set up the process of change in your family, the anger will show. Our studies indicate that angry remarks disrupt discussions aimed at serious family problem solving. One hostile comment leads to another and the outcome is a fight instead of a solved problem.(12) Selecting the right behavior in the first place is important in starting to change behavior. If you begin with the hardest problems, you are likely to be defeated. A good rule of thumb is to select problems that are not terribly upsetting to you or your adolescent. Save the ones that get you into fierce battles for last.

4. Select behaviors that happen at least two or three times a day. Learning to pay careful attention to specific behaviors takes lots of practice. Each day you will be looking for examples of the good and bad behaviors you want to change. It is hard to remember to pay attention to something that seldom happens, so pick a set of behaviors that will keep you on your toes.

Counting and Labeling the Specifics

So far we have discussed three main ideas: 1) most of us use stereotypes and generalizations to describe the behavior of people and what is going on around us; 2) if we use stereotypes it is difficult to recognize changes in behavior; and 3) tracking and counting specific behaviors breaks the stereotypes down into workable units. It is counting behaviors that will also tell us whether changes are occurring.

The idea of counting is simple enough. From the social learning perspective the process of change works best if everyone involved knows what is going on, so tell your adolescent what you are doing. Later in this chapter we provide an example of how to announce your intentions. Put the tally sheet where the action is. The refrigerator door is the most popular place. Having it right there is a good reminder for you to track the target behavior and mark it down. It also serves as a useful reminder to your children that you are working on certain behaviors needing to be changed.

As points are added to the tally sheet, gently label the behaviors as they occur. You might say, for example, "Tim, you are talking back to me again," as you mark the tally sheet for Tim's back talk. It is also important to label and praise good behavior. "Tim—thanks for turning the TV down. I appreciate it when you do as I ask." In that last example the parent gets extra credit because the behavior being tracked and counted was labeled (doing as asked), and a positive reinforcer for the behavior was slipped in. A reinforcer is a positive event that strengthens behavior (this is covered in more detail in Chapter 4).

Labeling the behavior as you track it teaches adolescents to be aware of their own behavior. This bold move, however, may involve you in lengthy debates about definitions, essences, and injustices. It is important to handle such confrontations briefly or the whole effect can be lost in discussions about what is, or is not, "back talk." For example, suppose Tim had responded by saying, "This is ridiculous—you call everything back talk." The way to handle this would be to say something like, "Maybe so, but that's more of the same," then make another mark on the tally sheet. Labeling behavior will not change it; this is simply the first step in the change process.

Tracking Some Typical Adolescent Behaviors

Begin by making a list of the behaviors you want to change. You and/or your spouse should take a few minutes to write notes on the things that are bothering you. Don't censor yourself at this stage. Just relax and think of the changes that would make life more pleasant around your house, or consider changes that would help your adolescent become better prepared for adult life. There are probably a lot of behaviors you would like to stop, and others you want to see develop. Write them all down. From this list you should then select one or two pairs of behaviors to track for the next week (this is part of the homework assignment at the end of the chapter).

Once you have a list, go over it a couple of times and mark a star next to each behavior that would be easy for you to track because it happens in your presence. These are the behaviors you can easily see.

Next, go over the list of starred items and place a second star next to the problems that don't get you too upset. You need to be able to stay neutral, or even friendly, while this process is taking place, so make it easy on yourself.

From the list of double starred items, select one or two behaviors to track. Make sure it is something that happens at least once a day, and preferably more often than that. As you make your selections remember that you need to define, very specifically, the problem behavior you want to stop, and the positive behavior you would like to see in its place. If you have a partner, go through this procedure together and try to include one behavior that is important to each of you.

Here is what a typical list might look like:

**Noncompliance/Compliance
  Being Late/Being on Time
  Chores (we have devoted an entire chapter to this topic)
  *Personal appearance (good grooming/poor grooming)
  Homework (good studying skills/lack of studying skills)
**Telephone Use (proper use/improper use)
  *Lying/Telling the Truth in Difficult Situations
  *Spending More Time With the Family/Not Spending. . .

Grades (good/bad)
**Talking Back/Being Respectful to Adults
Smoking/Not Smoking
Car Use (responsible/irresponsible)
Friends (hanging out with acceptable friends/being involved in a deviant peer group)
*Personal Habits (showering, combing hair, dressing appropriately for school, etc./not doing same)
**Teasing Siblings/Being nice to Siblings
**Bad Attitude/Good Attitude
Hair Style and Care (clean, combed, out of eyes,/dirty, hanging in eyes)
**Picking Up After Self/Littering the House
Wearing Makeup (excessive use/appropriate use)

Defining "Target" Behaviors

For the next few weeks focus your attention on one or two sets of behaviors. If you try to change too many things at once, you are almost certain to fail. We have provided a few examples of how to define selected sets of behaviors. Don't be limited by our descriptions, however, as each family has its own standards for behavior. Make up your own definitions. Discuss them with your spouse if you have one, or with your friends.

Make your definitions age appropriate. The expectations you have for an 18-year-old high school senior should be different from those you have for a 12-year-old who has just entered middle school. On the other hand, if your 12-year-old is more responsible than your 18-year-old, take that into account. Don't set your standards so high that they are completely out of reach.

Let's illustrate how this is done by considering the steps necessary to improve homework skills. The definition of homework depends upon the age and skill level of your adolescent. If, for example, your 15-year-old son is doing poorly in school, the first step is to "engineer" his environment so that it is conducive to studying: designate a specific time every day for studying; find a good place for him to study where other family members will not disturb him and there are few distractions (no television in the room, and so on); and make sure the basic materials necessary for studying are readily available (plenty of paper, pen or pencils, good light, and a desk). Your tracking sheet for studying behavior would look something like the following checklist.

Behaviors	Mon	Tue	Wed	Thu	Fri	Sat	Sun
Studying:							
Sit at desk 30 min.	Yes						
Start by 7 p.m.	No						
Books open	Yes						
TV turned off	Yes						
No interruptions	No						

In order to track studying behavior, you would record each of these components every day. All of these details may be necessary if your adolescent has poor study skills. The procedure can be streamlined for teenagers who already have good study skills. In this case, all that may be required is to ask them if they have completed the homework assignment for the day, and to occasionally check their work to make sure they are doing it correctly. If they are getting good grades let them work out their own details as to where, when and how the homework is done.

Telephone use is often a problem in families with adolescents. The guidelines for telephone use depend upon the circumstances in your family. With only one teenager in the house the problem is bad enough. If you have several teenagers you have the sympathy of the authors and a telephone that is constantly in use. Establishing a set of telephone rules that are carefully tracked can help. Mother Bell must have had adolescents in mind when the "call waiting" feature was invented. This makes it possible to get through when someone is already talking on the telephone. The problem is that calls can be stacked up like airplanes at the Chicago Airport. The net result is that the telephone can be tied up for hours. Setting a time limit on telephone conversations and using a timer are some good ways to solve this problem. The following is an example of a chart that could be used to keep track of telephone use:

MONDAY

		Telephone Use		Telephone polite	Answering # times
	# calls	time on	total time	yes/no	answered
Jane	2	45,35	80	Y	1
Dana	4	10,25,3,7	45	Y,Y	2
Erik	0	0	0	Y,N,N,Y	4
Mom	2	1,10	11	Y,N	2
Dad	1	20	20		0

Before you start a program like this you should sit down with everyone concerned and discuss the nature of the problem, and what you would like to do about it. Again, if this is an emotionally-charged issue in your family, do *not* start with it. But if it is a problem that other members of the family want to solve, then spell out the new rules and set up a tracking chart. Explain what you are doing with the chart so everyone understands what is going on. Begin by collecting a little data on the basics. The sample chart above illustrates one way of doing it in a five person family. Each person's name is listed along with a place for recording number of calls, time per call, total telephone time, the number of times that person answered the phone, and whether or not he or she was polite.

A look at this chart highlights some of the problems this family is having. There was a total of nine phone calls during a single evening, tying up the line for nearly three hours. You can also see that Erik answers the telephone more than anyone else, and that he has a slight problem with being polite. While Jane received fewer calls than Dana, she spent more time on the phone. Mom and Dad were only minimally involved in using the phone.

This way of keeping track of telephone usage may be too detailed for most families, but for other families it may be just right. Tracking three adolescents at once may be more than any parent or set of parents could possibly accomplish. One way around this would be to place the chart beside the phone and require users to record their own behavior using an honor system. If a system like this is used, the trick is to carry out random spot checks. Anyone who is caught cheating loses his or her telephone privileges for the evening.

If telephone use is a problem in your house, think about what you WANT and spell it out so everyone understands. The tracking process should emphasize what you want, and at the same time make it clear to everyone what you don't want. If your rules about telephone use need some fine-tuning after you try them out, add new rules or change them until you are satisfied.

While you are tracking, be sure to notice both good and bad examples of the target behaviors. This is one of the most important parts of monitoring. Good parents recognize and comment on the *good* things their children do as well as the bad. When your child answers the phone politely, say something positive about it; and if you are tracking that behavior, make sure you write it down. No matter how "bad" your teenager is, *do not* just write down the failures. Learn to look for the small successes and signs of improvement. It is important to demonstrate to your children that their attempts to improve are appreciated.

If you choose to work on the personal habits of your teenager, this can include grooming behaviors such as brushing teeth, taking showers, washing hands before eating, and so on. It can also include guidelines for appropriate dress such as wearing clothes without holes, specifying which shoes can be worn to school because they aren't too disreputable, wearing a jacket during winter time, how tightly or loosely clothes may fit, length of skirts, whether or not shorts and/or jeans are okay for school, and so on. If it's a problem for you, state what you think *is* acceptable and what is not, and then keep track of how often it does or does not happen.

Spending time with the family should be fairly easy to define. How much time do you expect on a daily basis? When do you want it to happen? Under what circumstances? You may want your adolescent to be home for dinner by six o'clock. You may also find it necessary to arrange for another hour of "family time" in the evening in the family room or living room, with or without the television on, (and time on the telephone doesn't count). It is probably a good idea to include a requirement that your teenager has to be reasonably pleasant, or at least neutral, during these times.

If you are tracking "picking-up" behavior you will need to specify which places you want uncluttered. Is it the family room or the living room that collects objects d'adolescent? Write down a comprehensive description of what you want—for example, books, clothing or other personal objects lying around in the kitchen, bathroom, or living room must be picked up and put in the bedroom, shelf or closet. It is important to track each room separately so that if your teenager is good about one room and not the others, some recognition can be given for the small successes. Remember that your task is to keep track of things in such a way that you notice the good behavior along with the bad.

Charting Behaviors

A blank tracking chart has been provided at the end of the chapter. You can invent your own form, or use the one included here. Artistic families use pictures, cartoons, and humor on their charts. Some of us are doing well simply to be straightforward about it. A good chart should have a complete description of both sides of the behavior you are tracking—the side you want to encourage, and the side you want to discourage. Beside each behavior there should be a space for every day of the week so you can make a mark each time an example of the behavior occurs. Don't try to track more than two pairs of behaviors at once until you have some practice under your belt.

Telling Your Adolescent About Tracking

By now you should have selected one more pair of behaviors you want to track and record. The next step is to let your teenager know what you are doing. We would like to emphasize again that the way you present this will have a bearing on how well it is received. If you can use humor, it will help a lot. If you can't use humor, at least be pleasant and straightforward about it. The worst way to set this up is to be sarcastic or threatening. Another way to create trouble is to tack the chart up on the wall as though it were some sort of edict from the king. Here's an example of a mother setting herself up for failure.

Mom: I'm sick and tired of your rotten attitude, and I'm not going to put up with it any longer, so I've set up this new program that's going to make you change. As you know, I've been watching whether or not you comply with my requests, and I must say your attitude stinks! You never do what I ask without making me nag you about it, so now I'm going to do something about it. From now on I expect you to do what I ask right away or you'll be sorry! Furthermore, just to make sure that you and everyone else knows about it, I'm putting this chart up on the refrigerator where the world can see how you're doing."

This sounds like an indictment by an Assistant District Attorney. The only thing missing is a police squad in the room, and a detention facility in the background. Even without adding an irritated tone of voice, the content of the message almost guarantees an adolescent mutiny.

It would be much better to say that you and your adolescent are having fights and disagreements over things that shouldn't be that hard to negotiate. Emphasize that the new chart will help both of you understand what is expected, which means you will not have to spend so much time getting on your adolescent's case about these things. This program will also help you to pay closer attention to the things your teenager is doing right. It may even be a good idea to include adolescents in the process by asking them to describe what they would like to change and showing them how to define, label and track behavior. This will reduce their resistance to the new program, and their input may be very worthwhile. Let's replay the previous scene using a different approach.

The Second Attempt

Mom: Alice, I'd like to talk to you for a couple of minutes.

Alice: What now?

87

Mom: I've been thinking about the problems we've been having, and I want us to get along better. I think that part of the problem has been that I haven't been clear enough about the things I expect of you, so I sat down and tried to spell things out. Here, look at this chart.

(They both look at the chart for a minute.)

Mom: For the next week I'm going to pay attention to these behaviors. I find myself thinking you're *never* on time, or that you *never* cooperate, and I know that's not true. As you know, I have been keeping track of your behavior and my behavior for the last week or so. One of the things I have learned from doing this is that I often contribute to our problems by being rude when I make requests. I also noticed that when I'm rude, you hardly ever do as I ask.

Alice: So what else is new?

Mom: Well, from now on I'm going to keep track of being on time and cooperating.

Alice: Where'd you get this ridiculous idea?

Mom: I read it in a book.

Alice: Oh, God. You and your half-baked ideas. What are you going to do with the chart?

Mom: I'm going to write down each time you do or don't cooperate, and each time that you are or aren't on time. I can't remember everything and I really do want to make some changes, so I'll be letting you know each time I see you doing these things. And I'll be writing it down. Feel free to remind me if I forget to notice when you are on time or cooperate.

Alice: I don't like this business about getting started within 15 seconds when you ask me to do something. What do you think I am, a trained poodle or something? What if I'm on the phone or right in

the middle of something. Do I have to drop everything to fit your schedule?

Mom: I will really try to be sensitive to the timing of my
requests. I know that I often interrupt you when I
don't need to. But, even so, when I do ask you to
do something, I'm going to write down whether or
not you do it within this amount of time.

Alice: And what are you going to do if I'm late or
uncooperative?

Mom: I don't know. That depends. In the next week or
two I'll be making more changes. This week I will
be paying attention to what is really going on with
these two sets of behaviors. After that, I will decide
what to do about it.

Alice: Why can't I just have a normal mother? Nobody
else I know has to put up with this kind of bullshit.

Mom gets up and calmly walks away. She considered telling Alice to stop swearing, but she knew there would lots of
opportunities to work on that later on. Her one goal during
this discussion was to tell Alice what she was going to be
doing over the coming week, namely labeling and recording
how well Alice does with being on time and cooperating. As
a parent you may feel the need to have the last word. Instead, you should be focusing on the changes you will be
making in the coming weeks. Words are not as important as
changing behavior.

Labeling and Recording Behavior

Every single time you see these behaviors during the next
week, comment on them as you write them down. Notice
when the behavior is good by being pleasant and reinforcing. Comment on the behavior you want to slow down or
stop in a neutral tone of voice. Simply say, "That's not coop-

erating," and mark it down right away. Or say, "You said you'd be home at five o'clock, but you were 15 minutes late." Then walk over to the refrigerator (or wherever you have decided to keep your chart) and record the behavior in the appropriate box. Do it right away or you may forget to write it down, or remember it incorrectly. Taking that extra step increases the likelihood that the change process you have just begun will be successful. Parental attention is still very important to teenagers, even if they don't act like it.

Key Ideas in this Chapter

1. Monitoring means seeing the big picture. It is important for parents to be able to answer the four basic questions about their adolescents: WHERE are they, WHO are they with, WHAT are they doing, and WHEN will they be home?
2. Tracking is the process of looking at the details of what is going on in your family. Tracking and counting specific behaviors serve the important function of breaking down stereotypes so that you can see if changes are taking place.
3. There are four rules for tracking: 1) be specific about the problem and its replacement; 2) start with problems you can easily see; 3) start with a relatively neutral behavior that doesn't get you too upset; and 4) select behaviors that occur at least two or three times a day.
4. It is very important to define the behaviors you are tracking in such a way that there is no confusion about whether or not the behavior is occurring.

Chapter Three Homework Assignment

If you have been doing the homework assignments in the previous chapters you already have some experience in tracking behaviors. The homework assignment for Chapter 2 was concerned with parental requests and the response of adolescents in terms of compliance/noncompliance.

This homework assignment allows you to choose another pair of behaviors to work on. Continue to keep track of compliance/noncompliance. SELECT one additional pair of behaviors to TRACK for the next week. DEFINE them carefully and WRITE them down on the chart. Pick ONE HOUR each day when you will be doing the tracking so that you can establish a routine. Make sure that you choose a time when you are likely to see the behaviors you will be monitoring. TELL your adolescent in a PLEASANT way that you will be adding these behaviors. LABEL the behaviors each time you see them, in a POSITIVE way for the good performances, and in a NEUTRAL way for the problem behaviors. RECORD them on the chart RIGHT AWAY. If you forget to do this for a day or so, don't worry too much about it, but try to do a better job of recording them in the future.

SAMPLE TRACKING CHART

Date _____ Adolescent's Name _____

Definitions for new pair of behaviors to work on:

  *Behavior to increase _____

_____

**Behavior to decrease _____

_____

Time of day for tracking: _____

Tracking Chart

Adolescent Behaviors	Day ____	Day ____	Day ____	Day ____
Compliance				
Noncompliance				
* _____				
** _____				

SAMPLE TRACKING CHART

Date _____ Adolescent's Name _____

Definitions for new pair of behaviors to work on:

*Behavior to increase _____
_____

**Behavior to decrease _____
_____

Time of day for tracking: _____

Tracking Chart

Adolescent Behaviors	Day ____	Day ____	Day ____	Day ____
Compliance				
Noncompliance				
*_____				
**_____				

Chapter Three References

1. Patterson, G. R., Reid, J. R., and Dishion, T. J. *A Social Learning Approach*, Volume 4: *Antisocial Boys*. Eugene, OR: Castalia Publishing Company, in press.

2. Patterson, G. R. *A Social Learning Approach*, Volume 3: *Coercive Family Process*. Eugene, OR: Castalia Publishing Company, 1982.

3. See Chapters 10 & 12 in Patterson, G. R. *A Social Learning Approach*, Volume 3: *Coercive Family Process*. Eugene, OR: Castalia Publishing Company, 1982.

4. Snyder, J., Dishion, T. J., and Patterson, G. R. "Determinants and Consequences of Associating with Deviant Peers During Preadolescence." *Journal of Early Adolescence*, 1986, 6, 1, 29-43.

See Also

Patterson, G. R., and Dishion, T. J. "Contributions of Families and Peers to Delinquency." *Criminology*, 23, 1, 63-79.

5. Rutter, M. *Changing Youth in a Changing Society*. Cambridge, Mass.: Harvard University Press, 1980.

6. Patterson, G. R., and Stouthamer-Loeber, M. "The Correlation of Family-Management Practices and Delinquency." *Child Development*, 1984, 55, 1299-1307.

7. Tomkins, S. S. "Script Theory: Differential Magnification of Affects." In H. E. Howe, Jr., and R. A. Dienstbier (Eds.)*Nebraska Symposium on Modification*, Volume 26. Lincoln, Nebraska: University of Nebraska Press, 1979.

8. Newell, A., and Simon, H. A. *Human Problem Solving*. Englewood Cliffs, NJ: Prentice-Hall, 1972.

9. Griest, D., Wells, K., and Forehand, R. "An Examina-

tion of Predictors of Maternal Perceptions of Maladjustment in Clinic Referred Children." *Journal of Abnormal Psychology*, 1979, *88*(3), 277-281.

10. Beck, A. T. *Depression: Clinical, Experimental, and Theoretical Aspects*. New York: Harper and Row, 1967.

11. See pages 283-284 in Patterson, G. R. *A Social Learning Approach*, Volume 3: *Coercive Family Process*. Eugene, Oregon: Castalia Publishing Company, 1982.

See Also

Patterson, G. R. "Mothers: The Unacknowledged Victims." *Monographs of the Society for Research in Child Development*, 1980, *45* (5, Serial No. 186), 1-64.

12. Wahler, R. G., and Leske, G. "Accurate and Inaccurate Observer Summary Reports: Reinforcement Theory, Interpretation, and Investigation." *Journal of Nervous and Mental Disease*, 1973, *156*, 386-394.

13. Forgatch, M. "Negative Emotion: A Disruptor of Family Problem Solving." Manuscript submitted for publication.

CHAPTER 4

Teaching Through Encouragement

This chapter discusses how parents can use positive responses to encourage good behavior. Doing chores, coming home on time, and basic compliance are adolescent behaviors that parents shouldn't take for granted. Providing positive consequences for these behaviors (both social and nonsocial) will strengthen them. Another benefit of using lots of positive responses is that it creates a nurturing home environment, which helps adolescents to develop self-esteem and good relationships with their parents. It is our strong conviction that well-adjusted and productive children come from homes where the parents are able to provide an environment that is both positive *and* contingent.

The homework assignments you have completed so far have probably improved the situation in your family. Setting up house rules provides structure and reduces arguing about rules. Parents can also make some temporary changes in problematic adolescent behaviors (such as noncompliance and back talk) by tracking and monitoring, and using requests that work. But these changes will not last unless parents learn to apply *consequences* for specific behaviors as well. On one side of the coin is discipline, and on the other side is teaching through encouragement. Parents can use discipline to reduce problem behaviors and encouragement to foster growth in positive directions. In order to be effective, parents need to know how and when to use both. In our work with families we have found it is best to start by adding positive consequences for good behaviors. This makes family members feel comfortable with the new program and builds a spirit of cooperation.

A Contingent Environment Is Predictable

The term "contingent" is a technical word which describes the relationship between a specific behavior and the response to that behavior provided by the environment. A contingent environment implies a "when/then" connection between what children do and how their parents react. For example, *when* your adolescent comes home on time (or before the established curfew), *then* he or she is allowed to go out again. Being late means there will be a negative consequence such as doing a work chore.

Many parents know how to use punishment contingently, but it is just as important to be contingent with positive responses. This is a skill many parents need to work on. Parents often assume that desirable behaviors will occur without encouragement, but this is simply not the case. When adolescents do something that pleases their parents, the good deed or behavior should be acknowledged. All it takes is a well-timed smile, a few minutes of conversation about a good grade received in algebra, or a positive comment when they help out by clearing off the dinner table (whether or not they are supposed to do it) to show teenagers that what they have done is appreciated. These reactions from parents strengthen desirable behaviors, and make an important contribution to the adolescent's self-image. Receiving lots of positive reactions from others makes teenagers (and adults) feel good about themselves.

A contingent environment means that when children are cooperative, their parents react in a *predictable* and positive way. In order to make the home environment a contingent one, parents have to pay attention to what their children are doing. When parents are contingent over a long period of time, their children gradually internalize the relationship between their behavior and the way people respond to them. When they do something good, people respond to them in a positive way; when they do something bad, they receive a consequence for their behavior.

Being noncontingent with privileges can create problems for parents. For example, if your daughter brings the car home with no gas and you let her use it again the next day, the implications are: a) you didn't notice it; or b) you noticed, but it wasn't important; and/or c) she has the right to use your things without being responsible for them. This is not what you want your adolescent to assume. Privileges should be *earned* by demonstrating increasingly responsible behavior. Irresponsible behavior should be discouraged by removal of privileges. This is a good way for parents to construct a world that has predictable outcomes for specific behaviors, and to teach their children how to handle responsibility. Another way to encourage responsible adolescent behavior is to notice and comment on their successes. Thank your daughter when she remembers to put gas in the car by saying something like, "You're getting good at putting gas in the car when you use it. Thanks for taking care of it."

In order to create a contingent home environment it is important for parents to control their own bad moods which may have little to do with what their children are doing. In other words, negative responses from parents should be reserved for those times when the children are doing something unpleasant or undesirable. Parents who are randomly irritable or moody deliver mixed messages to their children.

Using Encouragement and Reinforcement

A smile, a nod, or a word of approval are simple events that can change behavior. Studies carried out several decades ago leave little doubt about this.(1) Psychologists call positive responses such as these "social reinforcers." Basically, a reinforcer is something that feels good to the person receiving it. A reinforcer is like a reward, but the definition is a little more complicated than that. When a person does something that is followed by a reinforcer, that behavior is more likely to occur again in the future. Thus, *a reinforcer is defined in terms of its effect on behavior*. Reinforcement is the opposite of punishment—when a reinforcer follows a behavior, the behavior occurs more often; when punishment follows a behavior, the behavior occurs less often. Behaviors that are seldom or never followed by reinforcers tend to fade away gradually.

The impact of reinforcers on behavior is influenced by several factors. One important factor is timing. *Reinforcers that immediately follow a behavior are the most effective.* If you wait to praise your children for something they have done that pleases you, the praise is much less effective in encouraging behavior.

The message to parents is very straightforward. Look for the behaviors you approve of and provide a reinforcer *right away*. Don't wait for a perfect performance. Every time you see a small improvement or something you appreciate, say something positive about it. The nice thing about social reinforcers is that they work very well, there is an unlimited supply, and they don't cost a penny. Don't be stingy with your praise and positive comments. You are never going to run out of smiles, nods, or words of encouragement, so you should use them as often as possible as long as they are delivered contingently. In a very real sense, using lots of social reinforcement is an investment that will enhance *both* your own future and the future of your children.

Contingent Encouragement

A second factor that determines the impact of encouragement is whether or not it is used contingently. When parents respond positively to their childrens' behavior regardless of what they do, it weakens the effect on behavior. The key to using encouragement is to be contingent about it.

Adolescents who receive a rich supply of contingent encouragement from their parents tend to be highly socialized. They are responsive to small rewards such as smiles, head nods, or pats on the shoulder and are even more responsive to praise, or words of approval. If parents *seldom* react this way, however, their adolescents tend to develop a negative self-image and low self-esteem. These teenagers make up their own stories to explain to themselves why people don't notice their small successes, "No one cares. Even when I do something right, they don't notice it. So why bother—it's a lousy world anyway." In most cases parents are not aware they are doing this to their children. All too often parents fail to give their children the support they need and deserve because they are preoccupied with their own problems. But it is important to make sure this is not the approach you are using as a parent. There are many unfortunate consequences for children who find themselves in the position of relating to the world in this way.

By making the world predictable for your adolescent, it makes your world more predictable as well. When parents consistently reinforce positive behaviors and punish those that must be stopped, they can begin to count on their teenagers' behavior. Teenagers raised in a contingent environment are less likely to lash out at their parents randomly because they know they will receive a consequence for it. When parents are generally supportive, their children develop a sense of love and respect that makes them reluctant to do something that will hurt their parents or make life unpleasant for them. If you have your boss over to dinner, your adolescent daughter is more likely to behave appropriately if you have consistently shown her that she earns "points" with you by putting forth her best behavior on occasions such as this (if she's really good, maybe she will get to use the family car on a week night).

Jennifer Tries to Earn Some Extra Points

And this is our charming daughter, Jennifer. I know she's looking forward to meeting you...

The Cardinal Rule

Within families, the cardinal rule is YOU GET WHAT

YOU GIVE. Our research has consistently shown that family members who give the most unpleasant responses, also receive the most. The same relationship also holds for positive exchanges—those family members who give the most positive responses also tend to receive the most in return. This can either work for you or against you. If you generally respond in a positive way to others, it will make family life more pleasant. If, on the other hand, you are angry and irritable in the way you respond to family members, it will make family life unbearable. Since parents are really the ones in control, it is up to them to change the types of responses that characterize the exchanges in their families. Both parents need to provide good role models for the children by using lots of positive comments and praise at appropriate times.

Four Types of Noncontingent Families

Unfortunately, there are at least four different kinds of families that do not understand this concept. These are the "Misers," the "Warm Fuzzies," the "Nasties," and the "You are a Failure" families. We will present a brief description of each type of family, and point out some of the consequences for the children and parents.

In one type of family, the MISERS, family members never encourage or support one another. Living in one of these homes is like being in a desert—there are no growing things. For the adolescent, this is a barren world! The children in these families tend to have low self-esteem and feel that nothing they do makes any difference. Miserly parents are always dissatisfied with their youngsters. Their comments tend to emphasize what their children are *not* doing, or doing wrong. They fail to appreciate the fact that family members are not growing in positive directions *because* the parents have not provided much nourishment.

In the second type of home, the WARM FUZZIES, children receive praise, encouragement, smiles and hugs *no matter* what they do. Coming in after curfew is met with the same affable smile and attention as bringing home a good chemistry paper. Failing at school does not lead to predictable changes in the house rules about studying behavior. The children who grow up in this type of family also tend to have low self-esteem. While their parents are warm and accepting, the rest of the world doesn't work that way. These children have little understanding of what is appropriate or how to achieve success because their parents do not provide them with differential feedback on a day-to-day basis. These children often assume that their parents don't really understand them.

The third kind of noncontingent home, the NASTIES, is undoubtedly the worst to live in. No matter what people do, they are immersed in a cloud of sarcasm, disapproval, scolding, and sneers generated by other family members. There is nothing the children can do to reduce their daily dose of punishment. It is absolutely senseless. This sort of home environment is *very* destructive to children. Attempts to please their parents are met with scorn rather than praise, and they are quickly defeated. They are actively discouraged from trying anything new, or bringing friends home to meet the parents (who might say something terrible). The constant barrage of negative comments inevitably leads to a negative self-image and a great deal of anger. The cycle is completed when the children also become vicious. This makes it impossible for family members to feel close to one another.

The YOU ARE A FAILURE family is another kind of noncontingent environment that is destructive to children. The parents in this type of family are experts at pointing out the failures of their children. The timing of these statements is impeccable. When Greg earns an "A," his mother tells him about the neighbor boy's "A + ." When he gets an "A + ," he's told he needs to improve his social life. The children in these families tend to compensate for this by becoming very achievement oriented, but they are seldom happy with their accomplishments and neither are their parents.

These four examples of family types point out the importance of creating a contingent home environment for your children. If they were given a choice, most adults would agree that it is important to create a predictable and positive social environment to encourage their children's growth. But in many cases parents fail to do this and are not aware of the consequences. One way to make sure this doesn't happen in your family is to pay attention to your children's successes. Notice whether or not you are responding appropriately to what your children do. Are your reactions contingent? Are you consistent in the way you respond? Are you providing enough encouragement? Do you look for and comment favorably on your children's *small* successes? Do you try to control your own mood so that anger and irritability don't interfere with the quality of your responses?

It is interesting to note that parent/child patterns of interaction are repeated from one generation to the next. How your children will raise their own children is strongly influenced by the way you raise them, and the type of home environment you provide. Whether you are willing to accept the responsibility or not, your teenager is learning many of these lessons from you *right now*! Contingent or noncontingent, supportive or not—it's your family. It's up to you to make sure it works the way that you want it to.

Being a good parent means providing contingent reactions to adolescent behaviors that are so consistent your teenager can "bet" on them. We believe parental love is a very important part of the process of socializing children to be well-adjusted and productive adults who are able to form satisfying relationships with other people. We are simply making things a little more structured by adding the idea that *some* of the love parents give to their children should be contingent. Parental love also includes caring enough to use punishment to stop behaviors that place the child at risk for developing more serious problems.

Helping Your Children Grow by Accentuating the Positive

It is important for parents to provide support for growth and development. During early adolescence parents are actively involved in negotiating the goals for their teenager's growth; but during the later stages the goals are set primarily by the adolescent. One of the implications of this is that you may need to provide positive reinforcement for growth in a direction that seems *to take the adolescent away from you*. This makes it really hard to be a parent, and even more difficult to be reinforcing.

Growing is a slow and subtle process. Sometimes it seems so slow that it is difficult to tell whether the child is making any progress at all. Parents can see major landmarks, like graduating from middle school, or turning 16, but they can't recognize a pattern or direction in what their children are doing. How can you reinforce subtle growth that seems to have no pattern? During any given week your children may declare a lifelong interest in soccer, sign up for the school band, and sit in dark corners reading Gibran's *The Prophet*. Who knows where these new experiences will take them? In your role as supportive parent it is your job to provide encouragement and reinforcement for as many of these experiments as you can, and accept the rest with a good sense of humor and a willingness to be proven wrong. Incidentally, there are some instances where it is your duty to say "No," but we will come back to that later on.

Most parents notice enormous differences among siblings. The new studies in behavioral genetics suggest that our genetic make-up influences the kinds of experiences we find reinforcing.(2) Siblings share only 50% of their genes so there is room for large differences in what parents are asked to support. Some adolescents, for example, seem to thrive on excitement or thrill seeking, while others from the same family are more sedate. But it is the same parents who must somehow encourage each of their children as they experiment with radically different experiences.

Parents have to struggle to find coherent patterns within all of this adolescent trial and error. Even if you cannot see patterns at the moment, it is probably a good idea to support adolescents when they are trying something new so their experiences are not tainted by your disapproval (unless they are *clearly* moving in a destructive direction).

In both this chapter and the next we will describe some ways that parents can provide support for the positive behaviors we discussed earlier: a reasonable level of compliance, getting along with others, and carrying out routine responsibilities such as chores and school work. These are the primary skills adolescents must learn from their parents in order to become productive adults living on their own.

Types of Reinforcers

There are many different reinforcers that parents can use to strengthen adolescent behavior. Some of the reinforcers commonly used by parents include:

Social Reinforcers

Praising	Kissing
Smiling	Listening
Head nodding	Bragging about them to others
Attention	(in front of them)
Touching	Spending time together
Hugging	Doing things together

107

Nonsocial Reinforcers (also called "tangible rewards")

Money (allowances)	Extra TV time
Special foods	Having friends over
Use of the car	Spending unsupervised
Extra telephone time	time with friends
Points that can be	Other privileges
converted into	(transportation, later
rewards and/or	bedtimes, etc.)
money	

Social reinforcers are found in the behavior of another person. They are an important source of encouragement. Simply being a careful listener is a powerful reinforcer. Smiles and hugs are also effective. Two of the best reinforcers, although they are used very infrequently, are *praise* and *approval*. Our observations of normal family interactions showed that on the average, family members used praise or approval less than once every 100 minutes! In any case, all of these are effective social reinforcers that should be part of every behavior change program.

Parents who are trying to change behavior need to use nonsocial reinforcers as well, because they are more powerful. Tangible rewards produce fairly rapid changes in the behavior being strengthened. Nonsocial reinforcers have real value to teenagers if you select them carefully. The importance of nonsocial reinforcers was emphasized for us when we discovered that teaching parents with problem children to use praise and approval produced very little behavior change. The children simply were not very responsive to social reinforcers. Then we showed these parents how to use points that could be turned in for rewards and privileges, and this seemed to work much better. The use of tangible reinforcers also was compatible with our goal of creating a home environment where the parents responded to their children's behavior in a contingent manner. If you interviewed the children in these families you would probably find that being able to *earn* the things they really wanted was the feature of the program they liked the best.

When you first start using positive consequences to encourage behavior, it is a good idea provide the consequence immediately after the behavior occurs. As soon as the lawn is mowed, you should take the five dollars out of your wallet, inspect the job to make sure it has been done to specifications, and then pay up. This is especially the case for young children (less than 10 years old). With teenagers you might "pay off" at the end of each day. If your children are good about doing their chores you can change the program so that an allowance is paid at the end of the week. It is important to monitor their performance, give positive feedback by mentioning what they did right, and then provide the agreed upon reinforcer on schedule.

It is an art to select the right reinforcers. This is something you have to learn to negotiate with your children, otherwise the things you choose may not be what they actually want. Generally we begin by asking adolescents what they would like, and then we use their suggestions to draw up a "menu" of possibilities (this is part of the homework assignment for this chapter). At first you should help them select rewards that are reasonable and attainable within a relatively short period of time. Parents can use these rewards as incentives for good behavior such as compliance, or as payment for doing specific chores. After discussing this with your adolescent, and deciding what must be done to earn the reward, the terms of the agreement should be written down and posted publicly to eliminate any confusion. The agreement should be reviewed every few weeks and fine-tuned to reflect changes in what is important to you and your adolescent. With practice and a little creative engineering the paperwork can be reduced to a minimum. You might, for example, enter into an agreement with your adolescent daughter that if she mows the lawn once a week she can use the car on Friday nights as long as she returns it with a full tank of gas. This is an easy agreement to track—all you have to do is look out the window to see whether the lawn has been mowed to make your decision about whether she gets to use the car.

The kinds of rewards you put on the menu vary according to the age of the child. For middle school some of the more popular items would be staying up an extra half hour at night, being taken to a special event, having a friend over to spend the night, and *money*. Money is important to adolescents of all ages. For the older adolescent, going out with friends is also earned (first study, then have fun), and so is use of the family car.

Self-Esteem

Studies carried out by our research group and others have demonstrated that parental use of positive responses and reinforcement make a primary contribution to a child's positive self-esteem.(3) It is important for parents to use praise and approval frequently. Parents also need to provide support by actively listening and being involved in what their adolescents are doing outside the home. Support means that you let children know when their behavior pleases you. You also let them know specifically what it is about their behavior that you like. This helps teenagers build self-confidence, and makes a valuable contribution to the relationship between parents and adolescents. A good label for this parental role is "parent as friend."

As we mentioned in Chapter 1, antisocial adolescents generally have low self-esteem. This is also the case for children and adolescents living in homes where the parents provide little reinforcement or support.

In our treatment studies, one of the things that we noticed early on was that many parents would *agree* to be more

110

reinforcing to their problem child for specific behaviors, *but they were not able to do it*! We were surprised by this at first, but then we finally realized that some adults simply do not know how to be reinforcing. We had to teach them in role play sessions how to smile, make eye contact, and use praise and approval with their children without being sarcastic. Needless to say, the children living in these families had low self-esteem. Many of them probably thought there was something wrong with them. They didn't realize that their parents simply did not know how to be reinforcing.

Studies have shown that it takes literally hundreds of social reinforcements such as praise or approval to produce changes in children's behavior.(1) Punishment works much more quickly in changing behavior, and that is probably why so many parents rely on it as their main method for socializing their children. Nevertheless, helping your adolescents live up to their potential is an act of love that requires an environment rich in encouragement and reinforcement. In this case, slower is better because it doesn't carry with it the loss of self-esteem that accompanies the extensive use of punishment.

Four Rules for Using Reinforcement and Encouragement

1. *When* the behavior takes place, *then* the reinforcement follows (when/then). The WHEN/THEN rule for contingent responses implies that reinforcers should follow the behaviors you want to strengthen. This means you have to track what children are doing and be prepared to reinforce them. Giving reinforcement contingently does *not* mean that you should give fewer reinforcers, just that they should follow desirable behaviors. If you create a contingent and supportive home environment, your adolescents will learn that if they want something (whether it is your attention, the family car, or money), they can *earn* it by doing something specific. This is excellent training for the real world, and it

makes your job as a parent easier and more enjoyable in the long run. A little extra help around the house is always welcome.

Most parents try bribes and find that they don't work very well. Giving a child 10 dollars to get good grades next term is not likely to work in spite of good intentions on both sides. The 10 dollars would be much more effective if it were used as a reinforcer. This would mean dispersing the money over a period of time to strengthen each of the steps leading to good academic performance. During each step, *first* the child must achieve a specific goal, *then* you present the reward. Bribes put that sequence in reverse—that's why bribes don't work well with children who are trying to learn a new skill.

There are a surprising number of parents who give their children what they want without requiring them to earn it. These youngsters are never satisfied, and neither are their parents. The adolescents in these families feel they have a *right* to have their every wish fulfilled, and their parents find themselves wondering when the demands will stop and why they don't have any control over their children. Children attach more value to the things that they earn with their own efforts. If they receive something with no effort at all, they tend to take it for granted (the old adage is, "easy come, easy go").

Feelings of competency are derived at least in part from being able to produce predictable outcomes from your environment. One of the classic demonstrations of this concept came from a study of infants.(4) Each infant had a mobile suspended over the crib. For one group, the mobile turned but the movement was not contingent upon anything the infant did. This group of infants soon lost interest in watching the mobile turn. For the other group, however, the mobile turned only when the infants moved their feet in a certain way. This group soon learned how to make the mobile turn when they wanted it to. But the interesting finding was that when these babies made their mobiles turn, it made them smile (presumably because they were controlling their environment). Having the power to produce predictable outcomes from your environment is an important source of pleasure and satisfaction. A loving parent can take the time to make this happen by helping his or her adolescent learn the skills that make the "mobiles" turn.

2. Reinforce tiny steps. This is the rule that separates parents who are effective at facilitating growth from those who are not. Almost all parents say they reinforce their children or use rewards sometimes. But as you listen to them it turns out they *only* use reinforcers for major events or PERFECT PERFORMANCES!

Such parents act as though there is a limited supply of praise and approval available (like the miser families mentioned earlier), and if they give too much they will run out. If you ask them, they will say that getting a reward is like receiving the grand prize—once you win it, you *stop trying*! As it turns out, that is the way prizes and awards work in competitive situations. Once you have won the gold medal, anything short of a top performance is disappointing. You tend to lose sight of the smaller steps that are required to reach that goal again because you are focusing on the prize instead.

But in the context of families we are talking about growth, not competition. It takes hundreds of small steps to move toward a growth objective like losing 40 pounds, learning to play the piano, or getting into college. All of these tiny steps need small bits of encouragement to provide a "booster" for taking the next step.

Goals such as getting into college are accomplished gradually. The first step is to get good grades in high school. If your adolescents aren't getting good grades, then the quest for a college degree must start there. They probably don't *know* how to study, and because they are unsuccessful, they are not motivated to try. If this is the case, you might need to begin by helping them to develop good study skills.

To illustrate this, let's consider the problems experienced by 16-year-old Sam and his parents. Sam thinks he is college bound, but he is getting terrible grades. His parents promise him big bucks for "As," but he's never been able to pull anything better than "Cs." It would be much more effective if the parents would reward Sam for completing the steps necessary for developing good study habits.

The first step for developing good study skills is to establish a regular time and place for studying. Sam's parents should begin by rewarding him for sitting at his desk each evening for 30 minutes right after dinner. By the way, most of the people who learn to sit at a desk also learn to make use of that time. But when Sam's parents first tried this, all he did was to sit there and read *Rolling Stone* magazine. His parents kept their part of the bargain, however, and paid him for going to his desk right after dinner and sitting there with the TV off. Sam liked earning a dollar for catching up on the news about his favorite rock stars.

The next week, however, his parents added another step. Now Sam was allowed to have only school books at his desk, and to earn the dollar he was required to have the books open in front of him. After a week of this, Sam's parents added the next step. Now it was necessary for Sam to actually get something done to earn the dollar. Sam's parents established some academic goals which were small enough that it was easy for Sam to achieve them with a little effort (a certain number of pages in the math book, or writing several paragraphs of his essay, and so on).

The principle is to start with the *first steps* in learning a skill, and reward each small success. Most of us feel silly rewarding an adolescent for simply sitting at a desk—this is something that any child who is five or six years old could do. But this makes it possible for the adolescent to actually receive the rewards that are promised, and experience what it feels like to succeed. As new steps are added, the increments in effort and skill are small enough that again the teenager can succeed. This the best way to help your adolescent improve a less-than-perfect skill.

As the adolescent masters each step in acquiring good homework skills, the parents should gradually raise the criteria required to earn the reinforcer. At first, sitting at the desk was all that was required. Then Sam had to set aside his *Rolling Stone* magazines and have his school books in front of him. At step three he had to get something done to earn the reward. After a while he was required to get his homework *done* and do a good job on it. This slow moving process meant that Sam's parents had to be involved in tracking his homework assignments for a long period of time. Even though this takes a great deal of effort, it saves time and trouble in the long run because it reduces the nagging and bickering about late homework assignments and bad report cards. As Sam gradually improved his homework skills, his parents were able to reduce their involvement. When Sam begins to see his own progress and gains confidence in his academic skills, he may actually begin to enjoy the learning process. What this means is that doing well in school becomes intrinsically rewarding (that is, the experience itself is rewarding). This is how "self motivation" can be developed. But it requires attentive, patient and supportive parents. In general, competency experiences are usually intrinsically rewarding. The bottom line for parents engaging in this sort of remedial work is: HELP YOUR CHILD TAKE TINY STEPS, AND SUPPORT EACH STEP FORWARD.

Perfect performances are rare. It is not reasonable to expect your children to earn their rewards by doing what they have not yet learned. If you want them to be successful, then break long-range goals into small steps, and provide lots of support and rewards along the way.

3. At first, reinforce every time. This rule emphasizes the importance of being consistent. When you are trying to strengthen a new behavior, it is necessary to track it carefully so that you notice when it occurs. Then reinforce the behavior immediately, every time.

When you're changing behavior, it takes a lot of effort to get the process going. That's why you need to be particularly reinforcing at first, taking advantage of every possible chance to encourage small successes. After you've gotten the ball rolling and the new behavior is becoming easier for your youngster, then you do not have to reinforce it every single time. This does not mean that the overall level of reinforcement you provide is gradually decreasing over time. As new skills are mastered you simply move on to the next set of skills and provide a rich supply of reinforcement for successes. The process is like the old carrot and stick routine, where you keep the donkey moving forward by dangling a carrot in front of him. The difference here is that you don't wait until the end of the journey to let the donkey have the carrot. Instead, you break the carrot into pieces, and let the donkey have a bite every time you make it over a small hill. Each significant step forward earns another bite of carrot.

4. You get what you give. As we mentioned earlier in this chapter, our observation studies in homes suggest that family members get what they give (this is "The Cardinal Rule"). The family member who gives the most support also receives the most, and the family member who dumps the most unpleasant behavior on others also gets dumped on the most.

But this idea is not as straightforward as it may seem. The problem is that the events intended to be reinforcers may not be experienced in a positive way by the other person. For this reason, it is necessary to ask adolescents about the types of things they would like to earn for rewards. What is important to them? What kinds of things are unpleasant? You may be surprised at the way your adolescent responds to these questions, "Good grief, I didn't know that was important to you!" In the big picture of things, you get what you give in terms of positive and negative events. But the specifics vary from one person to the next, so it is important for you to understand what the other members of your family want, and for them to understand what you want as well.

The next chapter describes in detail how to set up an incentive program. The core idea is to build a point chart, which is the work horse of the program.

Key Ideas in this Chapter

1. Parents should provide lots of contingent encouragement for positive behaviors.
2. Four types of noncontingent families were discussed. In all of these families there were unfortunate consequences for the children and adults.
3. Both social and nonsocial reinforcers are important sources of encouragement. Don't be stingy with social reinforcers.
4. Parents who are contingent in their use of encouragement have children with higher self-esteem.
5. There are four rules for using encouragement and reinforcement. These are: 1) be contingent; 2) reinforce small steps in the right direction; 3) in the beginning, reinforce every time the behavior occurs; and 4) you get what you give.

Chapter Four Homework Assignment

The homework assignment for this chapter is to continue tracking and recording adolescent compliance. Now, however, keep track of compliance/noncompliance for the entire time you and your adolescent are home together. Every time you or your spouse make a request, make a mark in the appropriate place on the chart that follows. You should photocopy this form, or make up your own, so that you have a ready supply on hand.

The program is designed so that the adolescent earns a daily "back up" privilege for achieving a ratio of a least 50% compliance. This means you will have to select a reward that you think your adolescent will value. If you are in doubt, ask your adolescent for some suggestions, but make sure the rewards you choose are small ones (some possibilities were listed earlier in this chapter under "Types of Reinforcers").

Set a specific time for summarizing your data and providing the reward. Once this time has been established, don't be persuaded to change it. If 7 p.m. is the cut off time, don't extend it to 7:01 just because your adolescent missed the 50% mark by one response. If your adolescent fails to achieve a 50% compliance ratio by this time, simply state the fact and calmly walk away. Avoid becoming involved in arguments about whether or not it is "fair" that the privilege was not earned.

Try to be positive about this no matter what happens. Every so often during the day you should comment on the adolescent's achievements. Say something like, "Micky, you have complied with one out of four requests so far, and that's 25%. Remember, you need to get 50% to earn the special privilege of using the car tonight. There's still enough time to bring your score up to snuff—I'll bet you can do it!" You want your adolescent to succeed, so provide some encouragement and feedback before the cut off time.

If the criterion of 50% is reached, provide the reward immediately as promised. This program will only be effective if you are consistent about providing the privilege on schedule. Keep the charts in a file so you can see how your adolescent is doing.

COMPLIANCE/REWARD CHART*

Date _____ Adolescent's Name _____

Cut off time _____

The following privilege or reward can be earned by achieving a ratio

of _____ % or more: _____

Menu of privileges and rewards

1. _____

2. _____

3. _____

4. _____

5. _____

6. _____

7. _____

8. _____

9. _____

10. _____

Adolescent Response to Parental Requests	
Compliance	Noncompliance
Total Compliance = _____	Total Noncompliance = _____

Ratio = total compliance/total compliance + total noncompliance

Ratio for today = _____/_____ + _____ = _____ %

Reward earned today (Y/N) _____

Adolescent Response to Parental Requests	
Compliance	Noncompliance
Total Compliance = _____	Total Noncompliance = _____

Ratio = total compliance/total compliance + total noncompliance

Ratio for today = _____/_____ + _____ = _____ %

Reward earned today (Y/N) _____

Adolescent Response to Parental Requests

Compliance	Noncompliance
Total Compliance = _____	Total Noncompliance = _____

Ratio = total compliance/total compliance + total noncompliance

Ratio for today = _____/_____ + _____ = _____ %

Reward earned today (Y/N) _____

Adolescent Response to Parental Requests

Compliance	Noncompliance
Total Compliance = _____	Total Noncompliance = _____

Ratio = total compliance/total compliance + total noncompliance

Ratio for today = _____/_____ + _____ = _____ %

Reward earned today (Y/N) _____

Adolescent Response to Parental Requests

Compliance	Noncompliance
Total Compliance = _____	Total Noncompliance = _____

Ratio = total compliance/total compliance + total noncompliance

Ratio for today = _____/_____ + _____ = _____ %

Reward earned today (Y/N) _____

Adolescent Response to Parental Requests

Compliance	Noncompliance
Total Compliance = _____	Total Noncompliance = _____

Ratio = total compliance/total compliance + total noncompliance

Ratio for today = _____/_____ + _____ = _____ %

Reward earned today (Y/N) _____

Adolescent Response to Parental Requests

Compliance	Noncompliance
Total Compliance = _____	Total Noncompliance = _____

Ratio = total compliance/total compliance + total noncompliance

Ratio for today = _____/_____ + _____ = _____ %

Reward earned today (Y/N) _____

Adolescent Response to Parental Requests

Compliance	Noncompliance
Total Compliance = _____	Total Noncompliance = _____

Ratio = total compliance/total compliance + total noncompliance

Ratio for today = _____/_____ + _____ = _____ %

Reward earned today (Y/N) _____

Adolescent Response to Parental Requests	
Compliance	Noncompliance
Total Compliance = _____	Total Noncompliance = _____

Ratio = total compliance/total compliance + total noncompliance

Ratio for today = _____/_____ + _____ = _____ %

Reward earned today (Y/N) _____

An alternative homework assignment is to select another behavior you would like to encourage, such as getting good grades. Create a menu of privileges, select one reward from the menu, and write up an agreement that outlines what must be done to earn it. Break the goal into small steps that are easy to complete, and track the performance of your adolescent. If the program doesn't seem to be working, try substituting a different reward or privilege and breaking the goal into smaller steps. A little fine-tuning is often needed to make the program effective.

Alternate Homework Assignment

GOAL STEPS/REWARD CHART*

The Goal _____

Step 1. _____

Step 2. _____

Step 3. _____

Step 4. _____

Agreement for Earning Extra Privileges

It is agreed that _____ can earn privilege or reward

number _____ by completing goal step number _____ .

Alternate Homework Assignment

GOAL STEPS/REWARD CHART*

The Goal _____

Step 1. _____

Step 2. _____

Step 3. _____

Step 4. _____

Agreement for Earning Extra Privileges

It is agreed that _____ can earn privilege or reward

number _____ by completing goal step number _____ .

*A workbook containing additional copies of these forms (in a larger format) is available from the publisher.

Chapter Four References

1. The empirical studies on how positive reinforcement operates within families are reviewed in Chapter 5 in Patterson, G. R. *Coercive Family Process*. Eugene, OR: Castalia Publishing Company, 1982.

See Also

The general concepts relating to reinforcement and contingency are presented in Skinner, B. F. *Walden Two*. New York: Macmillan Co., 1948.

See Also

Skinner, B. F. *Contingencies of Reinforcement*. New York: Appleton-Century-Crofts, 1969.

2. Plomin R., DeFries, J. C., and Loehlin, J. C. "Genotype Environment Interaction and Correlation in the Analysis of Human Behavior." *Psychological Bulletin*, 1977, 84, 309-322.

See Also

Sears, S., Webber, P. L., Weinberg, R. A., and Wittig, M. A. "Personality Resemblance Among Adolescents and Their Parents in Biologically Related and Adoptive Families." *Journal of Personality and Social Psychology*, 1981, 40, 885-898.

3. Patterson, G. R., Reid, J. B., and Dishion, T. J. *Antisocial Boys*. Eugene, OR: Castalia Publishing Company, in press.

4. One of the classic studies about infants and contingent environments is described in Watson, J. S. "Perception of Contingency as a Determinant for Social Responsiveness." In E. Thomas (Ed.) *Origins of Infant Social Responsiveness* (Vol. 1). New York: Halsted Press, 1979.

See Also

The treatment procedures regarding the use of nonsocial reinforcers in families are summarized in Patterson, G. R., Reid, J., Jones, R., and Conger, R. *A Social Learning Approach*, Volume 1: *Familes with Aggressive Children.* Eugene, OR: Castalia Publishing Company, 1975.

CHAPTER 5

Setting Up Point Charts

A point chart is a contract that outlines the agreements negotiated between parents and adolescents. In a sense, it is similar to the contracts used to establish the relationship between employers and employees. But it is more than that—it is a kind of Bill of Rights documenting parental expectations, and the rights granted to adolescents for responsible behavior. Specifically, it describes *which* rewards the adolescent will earn for *what* behaviors.

You have already taken several steps toward setting up a point system. A previous homework assignment asked you to define and track two pairs of behaviors. One pair was compliance/noncompliance, and the other pair was left up to you to choose. The positive behaviors from these two pairs should be listed on the first two lines of the point chart you will be creating (a blank chart is provided in the homework assignment for this chapter). The homework assignment in the last chapter asked you to encourage behavior by

129

providing positive consequences for achieving specific goals. This is really a simplified point chart. What we are asking you to do here is to set up a system where the adolescent earns points for good behavior and completing chores. These points can then be exchanged for money or privileges. The benefit to using points is that it allows parents to work on several things at once.

The point chart is an organic instrument; it shrinks, it grows, and it changes from week to week. It takes practice and a lot of trial and error to develop a good point system. If your first few attempts don't quite work out, don't give up. Redesign the system until you find a way to make it work.

Nine Steps for Building a Point Chart

1. Write down the positive behaviors from the two pairs you have already defined and tracked (compliance, and so on).
2. Make a list of the chores currently assigned to your teenager.
3. Divide the list of chores into Easy, Moderate, and Difficult chores.
4. Select two chores in the "Moderate" category, and describe them carefully.
5. Break these two chores down into components.
6. Assign points. Points should be assigned for chores and behaviors according to the level of difficulty and/or the effort necessary to complete them.
7. Set the criterion. This is the number of points your adolescent must earn each day to be eligible for a reward.
8. Make up a reward menu.
9. Track the points earned daily.

Now we will discuss each step in detail (except #1).

2. Listing chores. There are very few household tasks that cannot be done by healthy children in their teens (or even younger). A list of these tasks would include the following: setting the table, clearing the table, doing the dishes, some cooking, vacuuming, dusting, picking up around the house, responsibilities for specific rooms (family room, bathroom, living room, and so on), doing the laundry, taking out the garbage, bedroom maintenance, feeding pets, running errands, and carrying, stacking, and chopping wood.

Teaching teenagers to do these chores is a good way to prepare them for life as adults. Before they grow up and leave home, adolescents should learn how to be competent in carrying out routine household duties. This does not mean they should be expected to do *all* of these tasks on their own, but they should learn HOW to do them.

During this first stage, list the chores you would like to have your teenager do on a daily basis (jobs that need to be done once or twice each week can be added later on). For a younger child (seven or eight years of age), a reasonable chore detail might take only 10 minutes a day; for an adolescent, it might take 30 or 40 minutes a day, with an extra hour or two required on weekends. You want to be careful not to ask too much. It's a good idea to compare notes on this topic with friends who have children the same age.

3. Establishing levels of difficulty and unpleasantness. Some jobs, by their very nature, are worse than others. They may not necessarily be more strenuous, just more unpleasant. Cleaning the toilet or cat box, for example, may be worse than sweeping the floor because it is a dirty job (or, as most adolescents would say, it's "gross"). The determination of whether something is easy or hard is also highly individualistic. Some youngsters take pride in keeping their bedrooms clean. For them it is easy to be orderly. Other children, however, let their bedrooms look like a hurricane

131

just passed through it and don't seem bothered by it. These children seem to have a great deal of difficulty being organized on a daily basis. For this reason, it is important to keep each child's personality in mind when you are assigning levels of difficulty to chores.

You may also want to divide up the list of chores according to your child's skill level. Advanced: done well without prompting; Intermediate: done moderately well most of the time, some prompting required, needs improvement; Beginner: done poorly, seldom done without repeated prompting, needs much improvement.

In our own family, each child was required to do at least one chore on a daily basis. The difficult chores were presented as an opportunity to earn additional points or money.

4. **Selecting chores.** Look over the list you have just created. Think carefully about which chores you would like to work on. If your adolescent has already been doing some chores, and is relatively consistent about doing them, select two chores from the "Moderate" category—these are less likely to be met with resistance than the chores in the "Difficult" category. If your adolescent has poor work skills when it comes to doing chores without constant nagging, start with two chores in the "Easy" category. The underlying principle is to select two chores that your adolescent *will be able to do* without much hassle. More difficult chores can be assigned after the adolescent demonstrates competency in completing less demanding chores.

5. **Breaking the chores into components.** This is an important part of designing an effective point system. Each chore must be described in terms of the components that must be completed. This makes it easy for both the parents and the teenager to know whether or not the chore has been done properly, and it eliminates a lot of nagging and arguing. It may take a couple of days of trying out the chore and revising the job description before you are satisfied that the system "works."

When you try to describe the components of a chore, go to the scene and picture in your mind's eye all of the aspects you think should be covered in order to do a thorough job. To illustrate how detailed you can get, we have broken down "doing the dishes" into 33 parts.

DOING THE DISHES:

1. Clear the table
2. Wipe off the table
3. Put chairs neatly in place
4. Clear own setting
5. Clear others' settings
6. Wipe off TV trays
7. Put away TV trays
8. Wipe off and put away placemats
9. Shake out or wipe off tablecloth
10. Sweep or vacuum around dining area
11. Put away miscellaneous stuff (ketchup, mustard, pickles, etc.)
12. Wrap up food to put away
13. Put the food away
14. Scrape off plates
15. Rinse them (for lucky dishwasher owners)
16. Load the dishwasher
17. Wash the dishes
18. Rinse the dishes
19. Wipe or dry the dishes
20. Put them away
21. Wash the pots and pans
22. Dry the pots and pans (use a paper towel for cast iron pots)
23. Wipe off the countertops
24. Wipe off appliances (stove and refrigerator)
25. Sweep floor (pay attention to the corners)

26. Clean up the crumbs in the dining area
27. Put things away (salt/pepper, mustard, table cloth)
28. Scour kitchen sink
29. Rinse out and hang up washcloth
30. Hang up kitchen towel neatly
31. Close cabinet doors
32. Wipe up spills
33. Turn out the lights in kitchen and dining room

The idea is to start simply, but be specific about your expectations. The more of these parts of doing the dishes that your children have mastered, the fewer you will have to teach them. If your adolescent is already doing a good job on the dishes, the description doesn't have to be elaborate. When your teenager is consistently doing a poor job, however, it helps to be more specific. In either case you must build on whatever skills your adolescent has. Select four or five parts that are new or need improvement and describe them in detail. Show your adolescent what you mean. Even if your adolescent is not responsible for doing all 33 parts on a daily basis (which probably wouldn't be reasonable), it is a good idea to rotate the parts of the chore he or she is responsible for so each child learns how to take care of all aspects of the chore. Gradually raise your expectations as you see your adolescent's performance improving; add points for doing more parts of the job and make supportive comments about the quality of his or her work as often as possible. Don't expect your teenager to tackle all 33 parts at once.

6. Assigning points. When you try to assign points for each job on your teenager's point chart, you may quickly find yourself acting as a judge for The Court of Appeals. The following rules of thumb should help. Short, easy jobs should get one point. Hard, complicated, lengthy, or unpleasant jobs should be assigned more points, accordingly. Weigh the chores and their components on your scales of justice. Talk it over with family members. Easy jobs don't carry much weight. Hard work makes a big difference on the scales. Adding points for difficult chores helps to make them palatable and lighter on the scales. When you've finished assigning points, the easy and hard chores should balance out. Your children will also let you know how they view these point values. If everyone wants to do the dishes but avoids bathroom duty, decrease the points for doing the dishes and increase the points for cleaning the bathroom until you have some volunteers for the job.

Total the points for each job and compare them. They should be equal if the jobs are of equal importance or difficulty. If one is more difficult or especially important to you, it should be worth a few additional points.

Next, consider how many points each positive behavior on your tracking chart should receive. Most parents provide one point for each instance of compliance and assume it will happen two or three times a day. Behaviors that only take place once or twice a day (such as being on time, spending time with the family, or dressing appropriately for school) may deserve two or three points each.

Finally, add up the total number of points your teenager can earn each day. If you had 5 points for one chore and 8 points for another, then the total for a perfect performance on chores is 13 points. Now add to this total 3 points for minding, and 3 points for spending time with the family, and you arrive at a total of 19 points for an outstanding performance.

7. **Setting the criterion.** The "criterion" is the number of points necessary to earn a reward on a given day. If the criterion is 12 points, and your adolescent earned 11 points, there would be no reward that day. To be eligible for a reward, the adolescent must reach the criterion.

It is *important* to set the criterion low enough so the adolescent can easily attain it, especially for the first two or three weeks. DO NOT require perfection—most families set the criterion at 50% to 75% of the total points possible. This almost guarantees that the adolescent will have some success right away. As a parent you *want* your teenager to succeed, especially in the beginning.

You will be changing the point chart each week, adding new behaviors, removing old ones, changing point values, and modifying the reward menu. Neither the point chart nor your child's behavior will be perfect the first week or two, so make sure you establish a criterion that is reasonably low, but don't go below 50%.

8. Making a reward menu. The point chart will only work if the rewards earned by the points are valued by your adolescent. Finding the right rewards is easy for some families, and difficult for others (a list was provided in Chapter 4). As we mentioned earlier, it is usually best to sit down with your youngsters and ask them what small rewards they would like to earn on a daily basis. Later in this chapter we will provide an example of a mother actually doing this.

In making up a reward menu, there are several principles to keep in mind.

1. The rewards need to be valuable enough to the teenager to inspire the effort required by the point chart to earn them.
2. Since they can be earned daily, the rewards need to be things or privileges the parents are willing and able to provide.
3. There should be several rewards the youngster can choose. Everyone gets tired of a special treat if they have it day after day. (Money is one reward that adolescents never seem to get tired of.)

Explain that you are setting up a new system to help eliminate the nagging and hassling connected with chores. From now on your children will be earning points for doing chores. If they do their chores without being constantly reminded, they will earn something of value. Tell your children that they need to reach the criterion score as a minimum in order to be eligible for the rewards each day.

Make a list of at least five to 10 possible rewards. The way you communicate while making up this list is especially important. You might introduce the subject by saying, "What would you like to earn on a daily basis for your work around the house? I'm sorry to say that we can't afford a Corvette on Monday, and a windsurfing board on Tuesday unless we win the state lottery. Let's think of some things that are small but worthwhile."

You might want to use "brainstorming" as a technique for setting up the list. Brainstorming is coming up with ideas, some of which will be good, and others not so good. At first, write down *every* idea that is suggested. Then, after you have a list, you can cross out the ideas that are not very practical. But when you are brainstorming, the sky is the limit. Don't make critical comments about suggestions—this stops the process.

You may be surprised at some of the things your children would like to earn. Children often value things that adults tend to take for granted. Here are some things that adolescents have earned as rewards: additional telephone privileges (one-half hour to an hour), going to bed later than usual, a driving lesson, permission to go out on a school night, use of the car, transportation to and/or from some event or place, staying over at a friend's house, having a friend over, having a parent spend up to an hour doing something with them (playing a game, going for a ride, doing some window shopping, going out for a soda, putting makeup on together, doing manicures together, working on a car together), being allowed to use the parents' tools or equipment (with or without assistance), borrowing articles of clothing (such as dresses, jackets, or shoes), renting a movie, having a friend over for dinner, planning and/or preparing a special dinner, and MONEY.

Adolescents love money. Even small amounts of money that they can earn and spend *without having to answer to adults* is gold to them. The key is that they can spend it any way they choose. Now is not the time to hassle them about bank accounts. That is something which can be negotiated later on. *Working Mother* magazine recently conducted a survey of 1,000 of its readers and found that in 90% of the families the children (ages 5-16) received a regular allowance. The parents in 70% of these families tied the allowances to behavior, school grades, or chores. Nearly 75% of the parents indicated that they were satisfied with the way their children spent their money even though the parents did not exercise control over this.

Every family has a different budget. Families with a lot of money can afford to be more generous than families on a very limited budget. If you can barely afford a weekly allowance of five dollars, you should focus on extra privileges or rewards that are less expensive. Your youngster will understand. Most adolescents are endowed with a surprising sense of what is fair and reasonable.

9. Track the points earned on a daily basis. Without sufficient tracking, the program will fail. Adolescents quickly become discouraged if they put forth the effort necessary to fulfill their part of the point program only to find that their parents "forget" to write down the points they have earned, or fail to provide the rewards on schedule. Even if your adolescent does something that really upsets you, when the criterion is met you need to pay up. Punishment should not be related to the point chart. It is better not to start on a program like this if you don't think you can hold up your part of the bargain. Set up a simple program that you know you can track on a daily basis.

We strongly support the contingent approach to allowances. Children have very few opportunities to earn money by working for it. They typically are not paid for their daily efforts in school, which is one of their primary responsibilities. Few of them have the time or ability to hold jobs in the community. Working at home makes good sense to them. Money is one of the most popular rewards. Why give it away when you can use it as a teaching tool? All five children raised by the authors grew up under the pay-for-work system. They are all hard workers, and you can count on them to do a good job.

The point program lends itself very well to contingent allowances. Here's how it works. Given that the child reaches criterion, each point is worth a certain amount of money. The money earned can be paid on a daily basis if necessary, but usually there is a payday once a week. Since each point has a monetary value that you establish, it is up to you to create a scale that fits your budget and beliefs. In the survey conducted by *Working Mother* magazine mentioned earlier, parents reported paying an average allowance of $5-$8 per week for teenagers 12-16 years old. The data are provided below:

		Age		
	12	13	14	15	16
Allowance Earned (Boys & Girls)	$4.87	$5.62	$6.25	$7.76	$8.13

From *Working Mother* (December, 1986 issue).

Using Back-up Rewards

Many families use back-up rewards. The back-up reward system is flexible and can be applied whether or not you are using an allowance for work or daily rewards. Each day that your teenager reaches criterion, money or a reward is still earned. The back-up reward is a bonus that is given for reaching criterion A CERTAIN NUMBER OF DAYS PER WEEK. For the first week or two, you should make it easy to earn the back-up reward (in the same way that you made it easy for them to reach the daily criterion). Three or four days of successfully making the criterion is usually good at first. Later, you can gradually raise the standard so the child has to make the criterion five days of the week to be eligible for the back-up reward.

If your teenager was not receiving an allowance before, you may be able to simply set up the point program on a work-for-money basis. However, if your adolescent has grown accustomed to receiving money with no strings attached, and now he or she is required to work for it, this new system will not be received very enthusiastically. In this case it may be necessary to supplement the allowance with other small rewards. These rewards can be cost-free to you. They can include privileges, (staying up later, extended use of the telephone, borrowing the car, etc.), your time (providing transportation, spending time doing something with or for your adolescent such as playing a game, or helping out on a project), or more freedom (being allowed to go out to a game, on a date, or go out an extra night during the week). You can set up the program so these extra incentives can be earned once or twice a week.

The Art of Reinforcing

One of the advantages of using a point system is that it places the emphasis on noticing positive behaviors. The point program is a structured way to remind yourself to talk with your children about their successes. Each time someone earns points, comment on it in a positive way and write the points down immediately. Your child's efforts to play by the rules warrant an effort on your part to encourage each step along the way. Some parents forget to say something positive about their children's successes, or they don't write the points down. Then they accuse their children of refusing to cooperate with the new system. If you are asking them to change, you OWE it to them to notice the changes that do take place, and to praise them for it.

Some parents are much better at this than others. Here is a list of suggestions that will help you to be effective in using reinforcement:

1. Be pleasant when praising. Show your approval and support with your whole being, your facial expression, your gestures, and your tone of voice. Don't overdo it, or act phoney. Make sure you are good-natured about it.

2. Specifically label what pleases you about the way the chore is done. This encourages them to do it again. Here are some examples of labeling specifics; "Thanks for putting your coat away as soon as I asked you to—you just earned another point." "Your room looks great! You made the bed, put your clothes away, and straightened up your desk." A less effective way would be to look at the bedroom that has just been cleaned, and say something like, "You're a good kid," and then walk away down the hall.

3. Avoid adding unpleasant "cabooses" to praise. When you add sarcasm to an otherwise positive comment, it ruins the effect. Sometimes it even starts an argument. For example, "You did a great job on the dishes. Why can't you do that more often?" Or, "Your bedroom looks wonderful. I thought I was in someone else's room." Or, "Thanks for doing as I asked right away. It's about time you started to shape up."

4. Check each chore as soon as possible after it is done. If the dishes are supposed to be washed 30 minutes after dinner is finished, remember to go into the kitchen and inspect. Go over the chore with your adolescent and write down the points earned right away (remember, reinforcers are most effective if they immediately follow the behavior

141

you want to encourage).

5. **Be sure to notice what is done RIGHT, even if parts of the chore are not done very well.** A little creativity is helpful here. Phrase what you say as if you are trying to catch your teenager in the act of doing something right. If, for example, the job of cleaning the bathroom is only about half finished, start out by focusing on what WAS done. Downplay the parts that were incomplete, or left undone altogether. The following dialogue illustrates how this might be done:

> "You got a good start on cleaning the bathroom. The tub is nice and clean, and the towels and washcloths are all hung neatly. You get full points for that. I'm giving you half points for the sink, because I can see that you tried, but there are still some goobers of toothpaste left in there. Next time you'll get them all, I bet."

The wrong way to give feedback on a chore like this is to emphasize the failures and downplay the successes like this:

> "I can't give you very many points for your job in the bathroom. You barely touched the sink. Look at those globs of toothpaste! Did you even do the tub? Well, I guess it's alright. At least you straightened out the towels and washcloths. Not a very good start. Next time you'll have to get your act together if you want full points. This program will never work if you keep doing your chores like this."

A point program will never work for a parent who gives this sort of negative feedback. If you can't be reasonably positive while using the point program, it is almost certain to fail.

6. **Set a time to go over all of the points earned at the end of each day.** A good time for this is just after the last chore is supposed to be done. Once again, focus on suc-

cesses when going over the chart, even when your adolescent fails to reach the criterion. The following is an illustration of how this might be done:

> "You earned 12 points today. You did a good job on the dishes, and I gave you all 6 points for that. I especially appreciated how cheerfully you did them, I gave you 3 points for minding, which is pretty good because you were batting around 50%. You earned 3 points for homework, by sitting down at the desk with your books. Tomorrow you could earn full points for homework if you remember to talk with me about your work. Also, maybe tomorrow you'll remember to take out the garbage, which is worth 2 points. You need 15 points for a reward. You're 3/4's of the way there."

It sounds easy, but it is difficult for most of us to find time every day for these discussions. It's a matter of setting your priorities to include this time with your children. If you want them to improve, you have to make time in your busy schedule to encourage them.

The point chart is a contingent system for teaching adolescents how to share in the responsibilities of family living. Parents sabotage the program by failing to carry out the contingent part of the program. Some parents provide the reward even when their adolescents have not done the necessary work. Other parents do not provide the reward when their teenagers have carried out their part of the agreement. *Do not attempt to set up a point program such as this unless you can follow through on your part of the deal.*

After you have worked on the point program for a few months, it becomes possible to simplify it until eventually the children receive a weekly allowance for doing all of their chores. This eliminates the need for daily conferences about the points that have been earned.

Setting Up a Point Chart

What follows is a "teaching drama" designed to illustrate how to get your own point system started. Charlotte, the mother, sits at the dining room table. The table is center stage in this house. The family's recent history is written all over it. There is mail scattered everywhere, unopened bills, mail-order catalogs, and a few advertisements. A stack of worn school books leans like the Tower of Pisa on one corner of the table. A half-open backpack containing a damp bathing suit rolled in a towel, a soggy PeeChee, and a dilapidated loose leaf binder are in the middle of the table. Some dirty dishes left over from breakfast are stacked in one corner. A glob of strawberry jam has captured the attention of an itinerant mosquito, whose corpse remains.

The house is quiet, except for some peaceful music coming from the radio that also shares table space. Charlotte is dressed in a pair of faded jeans and a comfortable sweatshirt. It is 8 A.M. on Saturday morning, and everyone but Charlotte is asleep. She sighs as she thinks about the task of setting up two point charts, one for Miles, her 15-year-old boy, and one for Shana, her 17-year-old daughter.

"This week I'll have Shana deal with the bathroom and garbage, and I'll put Miles on the dishes and pet detail. Hmmmm. Well, the dishes are pretty straightforward. Let's see, now. What do I really want done with the dishes? Maybe I should have them do the dishes together. That seems fairest. The only problem with that is they get into such hassles while they're doing it. Well, I could have them take turns from one week to the next. Then I wouldn't have to listen to all that kvetching. Still, it seems fairest that they should share the job. This week I'll divide it between them." (She sighs and gets up to pour herself another cup of coffee. Charlotte changes the station to her favorite Saturday program of acoustic folk music, the kind that was popular when she was in high school.) "OK, dishes for two, then," she sighs again. "One of them could pick up the dishes and wipe off the table, while the other one washes and dries the dishes. I suppose I should put the food away if I want things done right." (Charlotte sighs again, and sips her coffee). "So, this week Miles can clean up while Shana washes, dries and puts the dishes away." She begins her list.

CLEAN UP DETAIL
clear the dishes from the table
scrape the food scraps into the garbage
stack the dishes
wipe off the TV trays
wipe the countertops, stove, etc.
sweep the floor

WASHING DETAIL
rinse the dishes and stack them in the dishwasher
wash nondishwasher stuff
scrub the pots and pans
dry the dishes and put them away if necessary

Charlotte looks the list over thoughtfully. "Let's see. Does it take about the same amount of time to do both of these chores? I guess so. Now, what should I have each of them do for their other chore? I could have them work on their bedrooms. Miles' room needs attention—it's a mess. Or I could have them. . . hmmmmm." She jots down some ideas for each.

Other Chores
Shana—bathroom, garbage, living room clean up
Miles—personal habits, garbage, bedroom, homework

"The bathroom bothers me the most, and Miles' bedroom is pretty bad. Both chores should take about the same amount of time. I think I'll go for that."

Charlotte leans on her hand thinking about the bathroom and what needs to change in there to make life easier. Taking her pad and pen with her, she advances into the bathroom, and leaning against the door, she begins to take notes:

BATHROOM. Towels hanging straight on racks, counter around sink wiped dry, soap placed in the dish, laundry picked up and put in the hamper, floor dry, makeup in makeup basket, sink cleaned out (no goobers of toothpaste or scum); water on floor wiped up, bath mat hung on the side of the tub, . . .

"No, I think the bathroom chore might create all sorts of problems between the kids. Shana would have a fit if she has to clean up after Miles in the bathroom, even though she makes most of the mess in there. I'll work on that in another week or two after we get this running smoothly. Instead I think I'll try to do something about Shana's early morning behavior. That ruins the day for everyone. How can I describe that in a constructive way?"

She gets up and starts pacing around the dining room table. She thinks back to yesterday morning and the terrible scene that brought this problem to mind. She wonders why they have to go through it so often. How does it all start? Shana didn't get up until 7:15, and then she was bitchy beyond belief. Miles was in the bathroom and wouldn't get out the first time she snarled at him. Honestly, if she could hear how she sounds, maybe she would change. . . . Maybe it would help to set specific times for each person's bathroom use. She goes back to the table and starts writing:

RULES FOR THE MORNING: getting up on time without prompting from me (6:30 on school mornings); eating breakfast; leaving on time (7:30); being pleasant (no yelling, arguing, or nastiness); bathroom time between 6:30 and 6:50.

"Now what do I want for Miles? His grades are awful. How can I deal with that on a daily basis? Homework! I'll start there. If he would do his homework a little more regularly, that would help. I know it would."

HOMEWORK: sitting at a desk in his room for 30 minutes, with book(s) open, looking like he is studying, writing, and concentrating on school work; showing me his work or discussing it with me for five minutes (pleasantly).

"Now if I assigned points for these chores and responsibilities, how should I do that? Starting with Shana, she's the easiest, let me see. . . ."

The lists for each child look like this:

SHANA

WASHING THE DISHES (within 30 minutes after dinner)

Points	Behaviors
1	rinse dishes & stack in dishwasher
2	wash nondishwasher stuff
2	scrub pots & pans
1	dry & put away dishes & pots

(6) points possible

RULES FOR THE MORNING

Points	Behaviors
1	get up at 6:30, without prompting from me
2	use bathroom between 6:30-6:50
2	eat breakfast (at least one piece of fruit)
2	leave for school by 7:30
3	be pleasant or at least neutral to family members.

(10) points possible

MINDING

(1 ea.)	doing as asked; getting started within 15 seconds

MILES

CLEAN UP (within 15 minutes after dinner)

Points	Behaviors
1	clear the table
1	scrape & stack the dishes
1	wipe off the table, countertops, stove, etc.
1	sweep the floors, kitchen & around dining room table
1	put stuff away (mustard, salt/pepper, etc.)
1	take out the garbage if it's smelly or 3/4+ full
(6) points possible	

HOMEWORK

3	sitting at his desk for 30 minutes
1	no radio, stereo, etc.
2	looking like he is working
1	book(s) or materials out
3	shows me his work or discusses it with me (PLEASANTLY)
(10) points possible	

MINDING

(1 ea.)	doing as asked; getting started within 15 seconds

Assigning Points

When assigning points to the various tasks you have selected, look at each task separately. If you set up point charts for two children at once, try to keep the points fairly equal. If both children will be working on the dishes together, it would create arguments if one earned more points than the

148

other, unless one job was clearly shorter or easier. Older children should earn more money or bigger rewards than younger children for their points when the criterion is reached, since this is the way that allowances work.

The easier task for both youngsters in this family was doing the dishes. They were already doing the dishes, so this is a good way to introduce the idea of a point program without adding anything different in the way of chores. For this reason, relatively fewer points are earned for this job. The new job, and, therefore, the one that is presumably more difficult, is homework for Miles and morning behavior for Shana. Both youngsters earn more points for this. Balancing the points for each child is accomplished by trial and error. You could say that since doing the dishes is worth 6 points, you'd like the new behavior to be worth about 10 points. Assign points giving the most weight to the most difficult and/or most important components of the task.

Once you have assigned points throughout your chart, total the possible number of points that could be earned on a given day. The only complication here is guessing how many times you think your adolescent will mind on a daily basis. Flexibility is the key here. Assume the worst. Last week you kept track of minding for an hour each day. If you counted only one or two minding responses, assume that you won't get much more than that for the first week or two on the point chart. In the example above, each youngster had averaged two to three minding responses. Charlotte added 1 or 2 more points to make it easy to round off the total to 20. Rounding off simplified the point chart, which is a good thing to do. Charlotte set the criterion at 15 points, a nice round number that represented 75% of the total points possible.

After giving it some thought, Charlotte decided that Miles and Shana would probably be able to reach the criterion about three days out of the week, especially during the first week or two. They were already receiving an allowance for doing their chores (although Charlotte wasn't always good about paying them on time). Miles usually received about $5.00 per week, and Shana about $6.00 per week. The difference in allowance between Shana and Miles was necessary because Shana was older and needed more money. But Charlotte knew that if Shana received more money for doing exactly the same chores, this injustice would cause bitter arguments. She decided the best approach would be for Shana to do an extra chore like picking up the living room to earn the additional money.

The first step for Charlotte was to spell out what "picking up the living room" meant. She decided that the chore should be worth about 30 cents, so there should be three components to the chore worth about one point each. With a pad and pencil in hand she looked over the scene in the living room. Charlotte noticed that there was a lot of clutter, and things were out of place. But it didn't seem fair to ask Shana to pick up after everyone. Then she remembered a trick her mother had used to guard against litter in the living room called "The Saturday Box." Shana's job would be to put personal items left in the living room into a large box. The rule was that everything put into the box had to stay there until the next Saturday. Then after the general chores were completed, the children and adults could recover their things from the box. Charlotte liked this idea because it killed two birds with one stone—it gave Shana an opportunity to earn some extra money, and the living room would be much less cluttered if everyone learned not to leave their stuff in there. Charlotte looked forward to announcing this new plan. She wrote the new chore down on Shana's chart.

PICK UP THE LIVING ROOM
(within one hour after dinner)

Points	Description
1	Personal items placed in the Saturday Box.
1	Straighten magazines on coffee table, put newspapers in the box in the garage, arrange pillows on the couch.
1	Take dirty dishes into the kitchen and put them in the sink, put food away, etc.

(3) points possible

If Shana did all of the components of the chore every day of the week, she could earn an additional $2.10 per week.

Returning to her calculations, Charlotte noted that if Shana and Miles met the criterion three times each week, they should earn about $1.60 for their points; since they had to earn at least 15 points to meet the criterion, each point should be worth about 10 cents. This would work out to be about $5.00 per week if all went as planned (10 cents × 15 points × 3 times per week = $4.50 per week for a minimum performance). If Shana and Miles were able to meet the criterion more than three times each week, or if they earned more than the minimum number of points, they would actually be able to earn *more* than their current allowance. Charlotte decided it would be worth a few extra dollars to receive a little more help around the house without having to constantly nag the children about it. She knew the program would probably have to be fine-tuned after it had been in operation for a few weeks, so she felt comfortable about giving this a try.

Charlotte discussed the new program with Miles and Shana and asked them what they would like to earn as back-up rewards for meeting the criterion three or more days out of the week. Miles wanted a driving lesson (he had just received his learner's permit), and Shana wanted to stay out an hour later on Saturday night. These seemed like reasonable back-up rewards, so Charlotte agreed. Both children seemed willing to try out the new program.

Key Ideas in this Chapter

1. A point program helps parents to focus on the positive aspects of their adolescent's behavior, it also provides the structure for changing behavior.
2. It takes effort to set up an effective point system and track the adolescent's performance. Do not attempt to set up a point program unless you are willing to track the points earned on a daily basis.
3. There are nine steps to setting up a point program: 1) add the positive behaviors from the two pairs you are already tracking; 2) make a list of chores appropriate to the age of the child; 3) establish levels of difficulty for each chore; 4) select one or two chores to work on; 5) break each chore into components; 6) assign points for doing chores; 7) set the criterion for earning the reward; 8) create a reward menu; and 9) track the points earned on a daily basis and provide the privilege or reward on schedule.
4. There is an art to being a reinforcing parent. You need to understand what is important and valued by your adolescent to be good at this.

Chapter Five Homework Assignment

1. Make up a point program for your adolescent(s) using the principles outlined in this chapter. This will probably take at least an hour, so make sure to set aside enough time for this before attempting it (you can also divide the task into two 30-minute sessions). Do not include more than two chores at first. You can always add more after the program is running smoothly. Include the positive part of the two pairs of behaviors you have been tracking (such as compliance and being home on time).

2. Talk to your youngsters about the program. Remember to present it in a positive light.

3. Keep track of your adolescent's successes, and be positive in your comments.

4. Go over the chart at the end of each day, focusing on the things that were done right.

5. Provide the reward when the criterion is achieved. Do not offer the reward if the performance of your teenager falls short of the criterion.

POINT CHART*

Date _____ Adolescent's Name _____

Daily Criterion _____ Pts.   (Total Possible _____ Pts.)

To earn the weekly back-up reward, the daily criterion must be reached

_____ days of the week.

Selected Positive Behaviors & Points

1. _____ Total Pts._____

Subcomponents:

A. _____ Pts._____

B. _____ Pts._____

C. _____ Pts._____

D. _____ Pts._____

E. _____ Pts._____

F. _____ Pts._____

2. _____ Total Pts._____

Subcomponents

A. _____ Pts._____

B. _____ Pts._____

C. _____ Pts._____

D. _____ Pts._____

E. _____ Pts._____

F. _____ Pts._____

Reward Menu

1. _____
2. _____
3. _____
4. _____
5. _____
6. _____
7. _____
8. _____
9. _____
10. _____

List of Possible Chores

1. _____ difficulty level_____
2. _____ difficulty level_____
3. _____ difficulty level_____
4. _____ difficulty level_____
5. _____ difficulty level_____
6. _____ difficulty level_____
7. _____ difficulty level_____
8. _____ difficulty level_____

Selected Chores & Points

1. _____Total Pts._____

Subcomponents:

    A. _____ Pts._____

    B. _____ Pts._____

    C. _____ Pts._____

    D. _____ Pts._____

    E. _____ Pts._____

    F. _____ Pts._____

2. _____ Total Pts._____

Subcomponents

    A. _____ Pts._____

    B. _____ Pts._____

    C. _____ Pts._____

    D. _____ Pts._____

    E. _____ Pts._____

    F. _____ Pts._____

WEEKLY POINT CHART*

Chores & Behaviors (pts)	Points Earned						
	Mon.	Tue.	Wed.	Thu.	Fri.	Sat.	Sun.
Chores							
1._____							
A._____ ( )							
B._____ ( )							
C._____ ( )							
D._____ ( )							
E._____ ( )							
F._____ ( )							
2._____							
A._____ ( )							
B._____ ( )							
C._____ ( )							
D._____ ( )							
E._____ ( )							
F._____ ( )							
Behaviors							
1._____							
A._____ ( )							
B._____ ( )							
C._____ ( )							
D._____ ( )							
E._____ ( )							
F._____ ( )							
2._____							
A._____ ( )							
B._____ ( )							
C._____ ( )							
D._____ ( )							
E._____ ( )							
F._____ ( )							
Daily Totals							
Criterion reached Y/N							
Reward received (indicate menu #)							

Number of days criterion reached this week _____
Back-up reward earned Y/N ___ Back-up reward received Y/N ___

WEEKLY POINT CHART*

Chores & Behaviors (pts)	Points Earned						
	Mon.	Tue.	Wed.	Thu.	Fri.	Sat.	Sun.
Chores							
1. _____							
A. _____ ( )							
B. _____ ( )							
C. _____ ( )							
D. _____ ( )							
E. _____ ( )							
F. _____ ( )							
2. _____							
A. _____ ( )							
B. _____ ( )							
C. _____ ( )							
D. _____ ( )							
E. _____ ( )							
F. _____ ( )							
Behaviors							
1. _____							
A. _____ ( )							
B. _____ ( )							
C. _____ ( )							
D. _____ ( )							
E. _____ ( )							
F. _____ ( )							
2. _____							
A. _____ ( )							
B. _____ ( )							
C. _____ ( )							
D. _____ ( )							
E. _____ ( )							
F. _____ ( )							
Daily Totals							
Criterion reached Y/N							
Reward received (indicate menu #)							

Number of days criterion reached this week _____
Back-up reward earned Y/N ___ Back-up reward received Y/N ___

WEEKLY POINT CHART*

Chores & Behaviors (pts)	Points Earned						
	Mon.	Tue.	Wed.	Thu.	Fri.	Sat.	Sun.
Chores							
1._____							
A._____ ( )							
B._____ ( )							
C._____ ( )							
D._____ ( )							
E._____ ( )							
F._____ ( )							
2._____							
A._____ ( )							
B._____ ( )							
C._____ ( )							
D._____ ( )							
E._____ ( )							
F._____ ( )							
Behaviors							
1._____							
A._____ ( )							
B._____ ( )							
C._____ ( )							
D._____ ( )							
E._____ ( )							
F._____ ( )							
2._____							
A._____ ( )							
B._____ ( )							
C._____ ( )							
D._____ ( )							
E._____ ( )							
F._____ ( )							
Daily Totals							
Criterion reached Y/N							
Reward received (indicate menu #)							

Number of days criterion reached this week _____

Back-up reward earned Y/N ___   Back-up reward received Y/N ___

*A workbook containing additional copies of these forms (in a larger format) is available from the publisher.

159

CHAPTER 6

Discipline
Unit 1

Introduction

The purpose of this chapter is to give parents some guidelines that will help them use discipline effectively to stop or slow down unwanted behaviors. Nobody likes to be told to change their behavior, especially teenagers. Usually such demands are met with angry emotional reactions that seem to escalate into major confrontations. If you try to change the behavior of children by scolding or hitting, then things get even worse. While the types of discipline outlined here carry less emotional charge than hitting and scolding, they too can result in angry confrontations if they are used incorrectly.

First, a brief review of what we have learned about changing behavior. The preceding chapters described how behavior can be strengthened by using positive reinforcers (both social and nonsocial). Any behavior will occur less frequently if the reinforcement for it is withdrawn (this is

161

called extinction). Behavior can also be weakened or stopped by using punishment. Since both extinction and punishment work, and since there are problems with using too much punishment, then why not just ignore problem behaviors? By ignoring them you are withdrawing parental attention, which is a reinforcer, and this should weaken the behaviors. The problem is that parental attention for certain kinds of behavior is only a small part of what is going on. Reinforcers are received from many sources for behaviors such as substance abuse, temper tantrums, promiscuous sexual behavior, or old-fashioned avoidant behaviors like truancy, lying, and forgetting to do chores. This means that withdrawing parental attention for these behaviors has very little effect. Parents can only weaken behavior by ignoring it if they are the primary source of positive reinforcement for that behavior. For example, parental attention is a primary reinforcer for the whining behavior of infants and adolescents; if parents ignore this behavior, then the whining will decrease dramatically. Ignoring only works, however, if the parents can be absolutely consistent.

Discipline techniques (punishment) are necessary for controlling certain kinds of problem behaviors that carry their own built-in rewards. Smoking a cigarette, for example, is intrinsically reinforcing because of the physiological effects it produces, and it is also reinforced by the adolescent peer group. The good feelings and wild times that accompany drinking or using drugs also strengthen these behaviors. It is easy to see why it is so difficult to change these behaviors by ignoring them, lecturing about them, or by asking the adolescent to use will power to avoid them. If your children are "with it," their peer group may encourage them to give all of these things a try. No one wants to be a nerd. The physiological effects and support from the peer group make substance abuse behaviors particularly resistant to change.

There are certain kinds of avoidant behaviors that also produce their own immediate reinforcers. The next chapter in this book describes how temper tantrums often "work" for the adults and children who use them in family settings. Throwing a temper tantrum is a good way for some adolescents to convince their parents to let them use the family car on a school night. Parents who have temper tantrums when things don't go their way at home are likely to get what they want too. Other family members end up spending a lot of time "on tippy toe" trying to avoid repeat performances. Most extended families have at least one person who is known for having rip-roaring temper tantrums. It is also well known by family members that it is easier to let such people have their own way than it is to try to change their behavior.

It was also mentioned earlier that it is difficult to monitor or give feedback to children who have temper tantrums (this is part of the Antisocial Triad). If you ask them too many questions, they just get more upset. In the short run, it is almost always easier to simply give in rather than pressing the matter further or trying to change the behavior. In the long run, of course, giving in accelerates the behavior, so you can't win with this approach either. With this kind of weapon at their disposal, these children soon learn that they can avoid a lot of unpleasant activities that grownups expect of them. Helping around the house or doing homework is dull business, so they don't want to do it. Successfully avoiding doing something you don't want to do is, in and of itself, reinforcing. Antisocial children quickly learn to avoid almost everything they dislike—chores, homework, music lessons, and going to school. Longitudinal studies have shown that later in life these same children are also likely to avoid working.

The conclusion to be drawn from this is that there are some behaviors that can only be weakened by using discipline techniques. Once you have decided to use discipline, however, there are several things to keep in mind.

1. Even when punishment is used, behavior still changes SLOWLY. The kinds of nonviolent punishments discussed in this book will not work the first time they are used. Behavior will not change just because you use punishment once or twice. In many cases the problem behaviors may actually increase when you begin to use discipline because the adolescent tests the new system to see if you are going to be consistent about enforcing the rules. It generally takes several weeks of discipline before you see a significant difference in your teenager's problematic behaviors. Even after you are making progress, the teenager will wait a month or two and then try again to see if you really mean it. Then you will have to backtrack and repeat parts of the discipline process. The "Let's see if they still mean it," scenario may be encountered several times with each new target behavior you try to change.

2. BE CONSISTENT—Use punishment every time the behavior occurs. Just like grandmother used to say, you've got to be consistent. Parents with problem children use punishment, but they are not consistent about it. They nag and threaten a dozen times before they actually back up their threats and punish the child; and then they are often violent because they are upset and angry.

Once you decide to weaken a behavior, track it carefully, and no matter how tired you are or how many distractions there are, *punish each occurrence*. It may seem paradoxical, but if you only punish a problematic behavior every fourth or eighth time it occurs, this may actually strengthen it!

The decision to use punishment should be taken very seriously, and it is something you and your spouse should discuss together. It is important for *both of you* to agree to punish the behavior that has been selected. Discussing your strategy in advance is a good way to insure that you will

164

both be consistent about using punishment. Disagreeing about discipline in front of the child, or large differences in approach, will reduce your chances of success.

3. Lectures do not change behavior. Lectures about the perils of cigarette smoking don't carry much weight when it comes to stopping an adolescent smoking habit. Lectures are designed to make adolescents feel guilty about what they are doing; this is supposed to motivate them to do the right thing out of a deep sense of morality and responsibility. It is also an appeal to their sense of rationality and better judgment. This, in fact, is the alternative to punishment that is advocated by a well-known child psychoanalyst. Given that you have a close relationship with your children, AND they are already very well socialized, AND you are absolutely Machiavellian in your ability to induce guilt, THEN making children feel guilty might work. Most problem children, however, are not very well socialized, and parents are generally not successful in using this approach to weaken behaviors such as substance abuse and poor academic performance. It is also the case that using guilt too often and too well can result in a neurotic child. It is more efficient and straightforward to use some of the punishments outlined here; they have no such side effects nor do they require special skills on the part of parents. These punishment techniques do not make children wonder whether or not they are good people. It is neither necessary nor effective to tell adolescents that if they really cared about their parents, they wouldn't be sexually promiscuous or smoke marijuana. As long as the punishments outlined here are not delivered by an angry parent, they will have very little negative impact on the child's self-concept.

4. Punishment by itself is not enough. If there is little warmth in the relationship between the parent and the adolescent, then punishment by itself could lead to active resistance and guerrilla warfare. It is particularly important to make it clear to children that even though you are punishing them for something they have done, your love and respect for them is unaffected. However, this is not done at the time you are using discipline. Love and respect should be communicated at other times. Everyone makes mistakes, and even adults need to be corrected sometimes. *All you are doing is insisting that they change certain behaviors.*

It is our clinical impression that some parents with children who steal are very effective in their use of punishment. Unfortunately, this is the only sense in which they are skilled parents. There is very little love in those families and no sense of respect for each other, least of all for the child. The parents are so effective at using punishment that they "win" all of the battles in the household. The only way that the child is able to "win" the war is to attack the reputation of the family by stealing and being picked up by the police. In one case, the boy even stole his father's family jewels, which ended up on display at the local pawnshop! Stealing is something that parents have very little control over because they are not present when the stealing is taking place.

By itself, punishment is not good enough. Love without discipline is not good enough either.

5. Calmer is better. Punishment usually means that the two people involved are angry. As we shall see, it is possible to discipline children without either party getting angry. At first there may be only one person who is angry, but that person should not be the parent, and this initial stage does not have to last for very long. With practice and the right approach, the whole thing can take place without rage, temper tantrums, or hurt feelings.

To most parents, punishment means using a physical consequence like slapping or spanking. Eighty per cent of parents with younger children reported that they occasionally use physical punishment of some kind. About one parent in five reported using an object such as a hair brush when they spanked their children.(1) Many of us have been trained to believe that punishment means inflicting pain on your children when you are really angry about something they have done. The social learning approach to discipline provides several alternatives to using physical punishment. With a little practice, punishment can be used without anyone getting angry.

Punishment has bad connotations in our culture because of the anger that usually goes along with it. The section of this chapter that describes punishment techniques also discusses some ways to tone down the battles that tend to accompany discipline confrontations. If each discipline encounter becomes emotionally charged, then you will eventually stop trying. Even highly trained therapists turn away from clients who are stubbornly negative and punishing to them.

The more coercive the adolescent is, the more likely it is that your first few discipline confrontations will be emotionally charged and difficult for you. Even a nonproblem teenager is very likely to react in a negative way when you first try using privilege removal or a work detail as a punishment.

6. Punishment is NOT revenge. The idea of revenge is something left over from our tribal heritage. The concept of an "eye for an eye and a tooth for a tooth" may have been a practical way to resolve the eternal feuding that characterized the early days of our civilization. It is not, however, a useful way to change the behavior of family members.

The problem with revenge is that the amount of pain inflicted depends on how angry you are at the moment. The social learning approach takes a very different view of punishment. This perspective emphasizes the importance of using punishment *only when you have control over your feelings.* Furthermore, the amount of punishment used depends upon how quickly you want the behavior to change, not on how angry you feel.

167

7. Punishments do not have to be severe to be effective.
G. Paul conducted a series of programmatic treatment studies in which techniques were developed to teach psychotic
adult patients to stop assaulting ward personnel and each
other.(2) Instead of the usual consequence of being placed in
isolation for several days by a frightened and angry staff
member for a major assault, Time Out procedures were used
each time an assaultive-like behavior occurred. The small
steps leading to major assaults were threats, pushes, and
shoves. Thus, the new approach was to put the patients in
Time Out for a few minutes every time one of these behaviors occurred. This approach resulted in a significant decrease in assaultive behaviors. And even though the
punishments used were less severe than long periods of isolation, it was one of the only approaches that worked.

The use of Time Out, privilege removal, work details,
and point loss to reduce problematic behaviors in children
and adolescents is one of the most extensively researched
topics in social learning literature.(3) The general finding is
that the repeated use of these brief punishments effectively
weakens problem behaviors. In one study, for example, consistently using a ONE MINUTE Time Out for three weeks
reduced problem behaviors by 61% in a group of institu-
tionalized children. Increasing the amount of time didn't
seem to increase the effectiveness of the punishment. It is
using a *brief* punishment such as Time Out *consistently* that
seems to be the important factor.

A Note of Caution

Finally, it must be said that we are a little worried about
teaching parents how to use discipline techniques without
some professional supervision. Our concern is that some
parents who tend to have too much control over their children's behavior may use the techniques in this chapter to
increase their level of control by using even more effective

punishments. It *is* possible to have too much control. Parents can "crush the child" by using discipline at high rates. This overly effective approach can lead to a negative self-image, and neurotic acting out on the part of the child. The social learning approach advocated here emphasizes that positive reinforcement and support should occur MUCH MORE OFTEN than punishment. Discipline encounters should be reserved for one or two problem behaviors you have selected to work on, and should not constitute the majority of your interactions with your adolescent.

How to Do It

Use a Two-Part Definition

It has already been noted that punishment is very effective in reducing problem behaviors, and encouragement through positive reinforcement is an effective way to build new behaviors. Punishment can be used to turn adolescents AWAY from a behavior. It teaches them what NOT to do, but it does not teach them what they should DO instead. For example, punishment can be used to teach a child to stop acting silly in the classroom, but it will not teach the child how to be a good student. When you are trying to change the behavior of your adolescent, you will be most successful if you simultaneously teach what to DO as well as what NOT to do. For this reason there are two parts to the definition of any behavior you want to change—the negative side you want to slow down, and the positive side you would like to encourage. When you start to use punishment to weaken problem behaviors, it is also very important to continue using point charts to encourage the development of positive behaviors to replace them. In the case of compliance/ noncompliance, parents need to provide points for minding requests, and mild punishments for noncompliance. If parents do this consistently, the behavior will change.

169

Five Guidelines for Good Punishments

1. SMALL punishments are better than big ones. Parents are often surprised when we tell them to use small punishments. Many parents assume it is better to use intense punishments so the behavior changes immediately. This means using a BIG punishment, and that is a mistake. There are several negative side effects to using intense punishments. One side effect is that it makes the victim angry. When parents are confronted by an angry adolescent, they often start yelling, threatening, and sometimes hitting; but this is not an effective way to change behavior.

Another problem is that parents who use intense punishments save them for extreme behaviors, which means lesser infractions (which are steps in the progression) go unnoticed. This is almost like baiting teenagers—nothing happens when there is some evidence that they are drifting into a deviant peer group or hanging out in disreputable places; but when they are picked up by the police they are punished severely. Parents need to have punishments they can use for smaller events so that the larger crises don't happen. This is more of a preventive approach that teaches children to make their own discriminations about what is appropriate and what is not.

2. Using many small punishments is better. Most problem behaviors are bad habits with long histories. It takes a new history of good habits to gradually replace the bad. The best way to get rid of bad habits is to use MANY, SMALL punishments, and many small encouragements for good habits. If the punishments are small ones it is easier to use them *every time* the adolescent breaks the rules. If the punishments are too extreme (like being grounded for a month or physical confrontations), parents don't use them very often. This means that the parents are inconsistent in their use of punishment. Sometimes a problem behavior such as noncompliance results in a beating, but most of the time the parent ignores it or nags about it. When parents are inconsistent about the way they use punishment, the teenager doesn't know what to expect. It becomes a guessing game, "Are my parents going to let it go *this* time?" Using extreme punishments inconsistently is not a good way to change behavior. Be consistent, and use a small punishment *every time* a target behavior occurs.

3. Select a punishment you can use right now. Punishments should *immediately* follow the problem behavior. The longer the interval between the behavior and the punishment, the harder it is for your adolescent to understand that there is a contingent connection between them. You want the teenager to know that when he or she does X, your response will be to provide consequence Y *every time*. It may be inconvenient for you to deal with an unpleasant situation at a moment's notice, but it works better in the long run if you do. Punishments are most effective if they are delivered immediately. If you wait to punish the behavior you either get angrier because you keep thinking about the problem or, worse yet, you forget to punish.

4. Don't use threats unless you plan to back them up. This is a very important point. Parents with problem children issue lots of threats, but seldom back them up. On the rare occasions when they actually carry out their threats, they are so angry that they may physically assault the child. Parents should NEVER threaten to use a punishment they cannot, or will not, carry out. Using threats that aren't followed up is another way parents develop a pattern of being inconsistent. Threats to punish do not mean anything in terms of changing behavior, and when they are used too often it teaches children not to take their parents seriously when they say, "Stop it, or else. . . ." On the other hand, if parents use a punishment like picking weeds every time teenagers back talk, then when the parents say, "Knock off the back talk or you'll be spending a few minutes in the garden," the teenagers know their parents mean it. The practice materials that follow are designed to give you some back up punishments that are small, easy to use, and really work.

When you tell your youngsters to STOP doing something, only make the request once. Tell them what will happen if they continue the behavior. Deliver the warning in a neutral, not angry, tone of voice. If you explain why the behavior should stop, keep it brief (10 words or less) and don't lecture. If the behavior does not stop within 10-30 seconds, then use the punishment.

5. Limit your battlefields. Don't try to change everything that bothers you about your adolescent. Select one or two behaviors that concern you most, or that you feel are important to the long term well-being of your adolescent. Concentrate on those first. Think about the punishment you will use, and *plan to succeed*. When the problem behavior you have selected shows adequate improvement (that is, it is not occurring very often), add a new behavior to the list.

Many punishments have been used by parents over the centuries to change the behavior of adolescents. Not all of them have been equally effective. Our experience in working with severely troubled families suggests that good punishments should have all of the characteristics listed above. The next unit will provide some specific suggestions for punishments that satisfy these conditions.

Key Ideas in this Chapter (Unit One)

1. There are seven things to keep in mind when you decide to use punishment: 1) behavior changes slowly, even when punishment is used; 2) be consistent; 3) lectures don't change behavior; 4) use positive responses and warmth as well as punishment; 5) be calm during discipline encounters; 6) punishment is not revenge; and 7) punishment doesn't have to be severe to be effective.

2. Use a two-part definition of the behavior you are trying

to change—describe in detail the behavior you want to stop and its replacement (the positive counterpart).

3. A good target behavior for punishment is noncompliance (its replacement is compliance).

4. There are five guidelines for good punishments: 1) small punishments are best; 2) use many small punishments *every time* the rules are broken; 3) select something you can use immediately; 4) don't use threats; 5) work on only one or two problem behaviors at a time.

Chapter Six (Unit One) Homework Assignment

Make sure you complete the homework assignment for Chapter 5 before attempting to use the techniques in this chapter. We have found in working with families that starting out with a point program is best. If you begin the process of change with punishment encounters, your teenager is very likely to resist your efforts. By starting with a point program, you are focusing on positive behaviors and providing the structure for behavior change (the point system by itself will bring about some changes if you stick with it). Adding the punishment components described in this chapter (all three units) will give you a complete set of tools to use in handling your adolescent's behavior problems.

Simply rewarding compliance, which is part of the point program, may have helped to reduce the problem of noncompliance if you were consistent about it. But it is doubtful that this will take care of the problem. The homework assignment for this unit is to continue using a point chart like the one used in Chapter 5. You will still be giving points for compliance, but for this homework assignment another line has been added to the bottom of the chart so you can also track noncompliance. Remember to label noncompliance in a neutral manner, and then make a mark on the chart. In the homework assignment for Unit Two of this chapter you will start providing a consequence for this behavior. For now, all you need to do is to keep track of how often it occurs.

MODIFIED WEEKLY POINT CHART*

Chores & Behaviors (pts.)	Points Earned						
	Mon.	Tue.	Wed.	Thu.	Fri.	Sat.	Sun.
Chores							
1. _____							
A. _____ ( )							
B. _____ ( )							
C. _____ ( )							
D. _____ ( )							
E. _____ ( )							
F. _____ ( )							
2. _____							
A. _____ ( )							
B. _____ ( )							
C. _____ ( )							
D. _____ ( )							
E. _____ ( )							
F. _____ ( )							
Behaviors							
1. _____							
A. _____ ( )							
B. _____ ( )							
C. _____ ( )							
D. _____ ( )							
E. _____ ( )							
F. _____ ( )							
2. _____							
A. _____ ( )							
B. _____ ( )							
C. _____ ( )							
D. _____ ( )							
E. _____ ( )							
F. _____ ( )							
Noncompliance							
_____							
Daily Totals							
Criterion reached Y/N							
Reward received (indicate menu #)							

Number of days criterion reached this week _____
Back-up reward earned Y/N ___   **Back-up reward received Y/N** ___

MODIFIED WEEKLY POINT CHART*

Chores & Behaviors (pts.)	Points Earned						
	Mon.	Tue.	Wed.	Thu.	Fri.	Sat.	Sun.
Chores							
1._____							
A._____ ( )							
B._____ ( )							
C._____ ( )							
D._____ ( )							
E._____ ( )							
F._____ ( )							
2._____							
A._____ ( )							
B._____ ( )							
C._____ ( )							
D._____ ( )							
E._____ ( )							
F._____ ( )							
Behaviors							
1._____							
A._____ ( )							
B._____ ( )							
C._____ ( )							
D._____ ( )							
E._____ ( )							
F._____ ( )							
2._____							
A._____ ( )							
B._____ ( )							
C._____ ( )							
D._____ ( )							
E._____ ( )							
F._____ ( )							
Noncompliance							
_____							
Daily Totals							
Criterion reached Y/N							
Reward received (indicate menu #)							

Number of days criterion reached this week _____
Back-up reward earned Y/N ___ **Back-up reward received Y/N** ___

175

MODIFIED WEEKLY POINT CHART*

Chores & Behaviors (pts.)	Points Earned						
	Mon.	Tue.	Wed.	Thu.	Fri.	Sat.	Sun.
Chores							
1. _____							
A. _____ ( )							
B. _____ ( )							
C. _____ ( )							
D. _____ ( )							
E. _____ ( )							
F. _____ ( )							
2. _____							
A. _____ ( )							
B. _____ ( )							
C. _____ ( )							
D. _____ ( )							
E. _____ ( )							
F. _____ ( )							
Behaviors							
1. _____							
A. _____ ( )							
B. _____ ( )							
C. _____ ( )							
D. _____ ( )							
E. _____ ( )							
F. _____ ( )							
2. _____							
A. _____ ( )							
B. _____ ( )							
C. _____ ( )							
D. _____ ( )							
E. _____ ( )							
F. _____ ( )							
Noncompliance							
Daily Totals							
Criterion reached Y/N							
Reward received (indicate menu #)							

Number of days criterion reached this week _____
Back-up reward earned Y/N ___ Back-up reward received Y/N ___

MODIFIED WEEKLY POINT CHART*

Chores & Behaviors (pts.)	Points Earned						
	Mon.	Tue.	Wed.	Thu.	Fri.	Sat.	Sun.
Chores							
1. _____							
A. _____ ( )							
B. _____ ( )							
C. _____ ( )							
D. _____ ( )							
E. _____ ( )							
F. _____ ( )							
2. _____							
A. _____ ( )							
B. _____ ( )							
C. _____ ( )							
D. _____ ( )							
E. _____ ( )							
F. _____ ( )							
Behaviors							
1. _____							
A. _____ ( )							
B. _____ ( )							
C. _____ ( )							
D. _____ ( )							
E. _____ ( )							
F. _____ ( )							
2. _____							
A. _____ ( )							
B. _____ ( )							
C. _____ ( )							
D. _____ ( )							
E. _____ ( )							
F. _____ ( )							
Noncompliance							
_____							
Daily Totals							
Criterion reached Y/N							
Reward received (indicate menu #)							

Number of days criterion reached this week _____

Back-up reward earned Y/N ___   Back-up reward received Y/N ___

*A workbook containing additional copies of these forms (in a larger format) is available from the publisher.

Discipline
Unit 2

The All Time Star in the Punishment Hall of Fame: The Five-Minute Work Chore

For parents with adolescents, the five-minute work chore is clearly the punishment of choice. Suppose, for example, you have told your adolescent daughter to stop teasing her little brother, and her reaction is an angry speech on the ignorance of parents in general, and you in particular. You have noticed that this is beginning to happen more often, and you can see her trying it out on others. Apparently mouthing off has worked for your daughter in the past, and you decide to do something about it. This behavior is selected as the target for a behavior change program. Start by walking around your house with a pad of paper and a pencil and write down the little jobs that would take about five minutes of work to complete (some suggestions are provided in Appendix 2). Have the list ready. You will also need a back-up contingency ready in case your daughter storms out of the house and tells you to take your work detail and shove it.

Actually putting a behavior change program into practice requires covering so many lists of do's and don'ts that reading about it would be tedious. Instead, we have decided to show you how to do this by including a teaching drama that features a parent involved in making a behavior change program work. The mother in this example, Ida, and her daughter, Carole, are made up of bits and pieces of ourselves, our family, our friends, and our clients. Ida makes some mistakes in setting up the program just as most parents do, but with some refinements she succeeds.

Act I: Ida the Irritable

The Scene. Ida, the mother, has just come home from work. She arrives a little later than usual because she had to run several errands on the way home. She also had to stop at the gas station to fill up the car because her daughter, Carole, borrowed it the night before and returned it empty. The house is dark and cold. Ida sets an armload of stuff on the table and sighs deeply, feeling completely alone in the world and a bit too tired to cope with the scene she knows is about to unfold. Yesterday's dishes are heaped in the sink, and the "ants in residence" are working on the pieces of crusted food on the countertop. Carole was supposed to do the dishes since this is her regular chore. Instead, she is upstairs in her bedroom finishing an art project for school. Her radio is broadcasting the top 40 hits throughout the house. Ida begins to ascend the stairs with a heavy tread, and a mood to match.

It seems that Carole has also had a terrible day in school. She saw her boyfriend exchanging notes with her arch rival, who Carole believes is more beautiful and talented than she is. Then she had an argument with her best friend who defended Carole's boyfriend. When the teacher called on her in French class, she made a complete fool of herself, and the class laughed at her. To top things off, she started her period in the middle of gym class. Needless to say, Carole was in one of her worst moods.

Ida: (As she nears the top of the stairs, she can feel herself becoming increasingly angry at Carole's irresponsibility. An argument is not what she needs right now. She knocks on the door and lets herself in before Carole has a chance to answer. Her raid on Carole begins with an attack on the radio. She gathers her strength and yells over the top of the music.) Damn it Carole, turn that thing down!

Carole: (She looks up from her desk, where she is attempting to complete a project for art class that was due last week. She sighs.) Oh no, here we go again.

Ida: (Standing rigidly in the doorway, she is an imposing figure with her face flushed, her arms crossed, and her mouth pursed in anger.) Don't give me a bunch of back talk. Turn that goddamned radio off right now!

Carole: Alright, alright, alright. Keep your pants on. (She turns it off.)

Ida: Don't you get smart with me. I'm sick of having to put up with your rotten attitude. It would be nice if you would do something useful for a change. All you ever do is think of yourself, and worry about your own little world.

Carole: Don't give me that shit! (She yells as she slams her book closed.) You don't do a goddamned thing but work, stuff your face, and go out with that jerk you call a boyfriend.

Ida: (pointing a finger at Carole) You leave him out of this, young lady. And knock off the swearing. You sound like an old whore.

181

Carole: (tauntingly) Well look who's talking. I must have picked it up from you.

Ida: You better shut up and get downstairs and clean up that kitchen right away before I do something that I regret later.

Carole: (whining loudly) But MOM, I'm busy working on a school project. I suppose you want me to drop it like it isn't important, and go down and do your work. You *never* do the dishes around here.

Ida: How can you say I don't do anything around here? (Her voice sounds defeated.) Do you think I do that miserable job day after day for my health? Do you? NO! I do it to keep this household going, and to put expensive clothes on your back so that you won't feel left out. And all I get in return is a bunch of flack from you when I ask you to help out. Who do you think does the shopping around here, the laundry, the. . ."

Carole: (interrupting her mother) And I suppose I do nothing, nothing at all?

Ida: Not without giving me a hassle about it.

Commentary

The battle goes on. The dishes stay piled in the sink, dinner is not made, and Carole's art project goes unfinished. Both Carole and Ida end up with knots in their stomachs, tears streaming down their faces, and hatred in their hearts for the other person. This is the tragic end to a terrible day for both of them. Instead of helping each other with their problems, all of their energy has gone into making one another feel miserable, and they have been very successful.

The net result is that nothing changed. The increase in misery did not serve any purpose at all. When Ida comes home from work tomorrow, there is a good chance that the dishes will be piled in the sink, and Carole will be sitting in her room listening to the top 40. What follows is another way of handling the situation that reduces the chance that Ida will continue to be greeted by a small mountain of dirty dishes when she comes home from work.

Act II: Ida the Indomitable (same cast)

Ida: (She enters the kitchen after the same horrible day at work, and begins talking to herself.) What a mess. Carole hasn't done the dishes again! (She takes three deep breaths to calm herself.) I'd better stay calm or we'll just have a fight, nothing will be accomplished, and another miserable evening will be my reward for trying to get her to do the dishes. Calm yourself, old girl. You don't want to get your blood pressure up. I'll calmly ask her to do the dishes now. I wonder if I can do it without making any sarcastic comments or long lectures on the irresponsibility of teenagers. Maybe she's feeling rotten, too. I suppose I could start out pleasantly, and ask her about her day at school. (Ida closes her eyes and visualizes Carole describing her day, and the conversation that follows.) Then, I'll ask her to help me clean up the kitchen. I'll ask nicely, say please and all that crap. And if she gives me a bunch of back talk about it, I'll make her clean out the toilet—it could use a brush up.

(Taking three more deep breaths to calm herself, Ida ascends the stairs.)

Commentary

The scene described above demonstrates the importance of planning discipline confrontations ahead of time. Responding spontaneously and allowing your anger to show does not place you in the driver's seat. Instead, you end up bouncing around like a ping pong ball that is outside of your control. Rule #1 is to CALM YOURSELF before initiating a discipline confrontation. Taking some long, slow breaths helps. It also helps to stop for a few moments and think about what it is you are trying to accomplish, and how you should proceed.

Rule #2 is to calmly USE A CONSEQUENCE FOR BACK TALK early in the discussion. Don't bother trying to "win" by arguing and confronting the adolescent with past sins, and don't wait until the battle escalates. If you do get carried away and become angry, then stop the confrontation and deal with it later. If you are angry, you are more likely to hurt one another than to negotiate any meaningful changes in behavior.

Act II (continued)

Ida: (She arrives at the top of the stairs in a relatively calm state of mind, considering the circumstances. She knocks on the door and waits for Carole to acknowledge. As she enters the room, she manages a little smile.) Hi, honey, how was your day today?

Carole: Oh, hi mom. (She looks up from the project on her desk.) You don't really want to know.

Ida: Why is that? (She puts her arm around Carole's shoulder.)

Carole: It was awful. . . . (She launches into a description of her misfortunes. Ida sits on the side of her bed and listens sympathetically. At the appropriate times, she prompts Carole for more details about the events of the day, and makes some remarks to show that she understands and is concerned about Carole. When Carole is finished, Ida gets up and walks over to the desk to look at Carole's art project. She is drawing the face of a cat in pencil. Carole's work is very good.)

Ida: Is that Penelope? (Carole nods.) I don't know where you get your artistic talent. It sure doesn't come from my side of the family. I wish I could do that. Is this a project for school?

Carole: Yeah, but it's a little late. I have to finish it tonight or else Mr. Ashton said he won't accept it.

Ida: Hmmm, it sounds like you're going to be busy for a while tonight. But you know, I could use a little help in the kitchen so that I can make dinner. Could you take a break from this for a few minutes? (She pats Carole on the back.) Then you can come back up here and finish your project while I cook.

Carole: Not now, Mom. (She replies in a whiny tone of voice.) I'm almost done, and I know exactly how I want to finish it. If I stop now, I'll lose my momentum. Art isn't the kind of thing you can turn on or off like a water faucet.

Ida: (This almost stops Ida, because it's a convincing argument, but she carries on because the principle is to teach Carole to take care of her responsibilities at home as well as at school. Carole is late on her art project. She is also neglecting her work at home. Ida decides not to say anything about this because it would mean getting into her usual lecture mode. Instead she remembers her plan and proceeds.) Well, I need to have you do the dishes NOW. (Ida pats Carole on the back again.)

Carole: M-o-o-m, not n-o-w! (Carole's voice becomes more animated.) I'll do the dishes after supper, I promise!

Ida: Now, Carole, or there will be a work chore as well. The toilet could use a good cleaning.

Tearfully, Carole storms past her mother, down the stairs, and into the kitchen. Ida gives Carole a minute or so before she goes down to her own bedroom, where she takes some time to sit down in a chair and scan the front page of the newspaper, a luxury she seldom has time for. This gives her a chance to calm down again, and it provides Carole with the space she needs to do her work. For them to be in the kitchen together at this point would almost guarantee a conflict.

Commentary

Ida used a relatively advanced technique in the second act that we will discuss in a moment. If Carole fails to carry out her mother's request, she knows it will cost her an additional work detail and/or maybe the loss of a privilege, and she will still have to clean the kitchen. In this scene, the mother did not have to add the work chore—she had already set the stage for success by creating a positive environment. How did Ida do that? Take a few minutes to write down the things you noticed.

Ida was friendly. She knocked on the door and waited for an answer instead of storming in. She smiled when she entered the room, and asked Carole about her day. She showed Carole that she was concerned about her problems by asking for more details and making some sympathetic comments. She praised Carole's art work, and did not make any disparaging remarks about it being late. She also used good timing in making her request about doing the dishes, and she suggested that Carole could return to her art project after the dishes were done. When Carole complained about that, Ida calmly restated her request. After the next complaint, Ida announced that a work chore would be forthcoming unless Carole complied immediately with the request. If Ida had said something critical or negative, or had become angry and confrontive, this would have started a fight.

Some people would read this example and get hung up on the fact that Carole's behavior wasn't perfect. They would expect Carole to comply immediately and cheerfully to her mother's reasonable request (after all, Carole knew she was supposed to do the dishes). But it is important to keep in mind that what Ida wanted was to have Carole do the dishes. Carole doesn't need to love doing the dishes, or even have a good attitude about it. Ida can work on Carole's attitude later. It works best to focus on changing only one behavior at a time. In the present situation it was getting the dishes done that was the issue.

One of the important things Ida did in the scene above was to give Carole plenty of personal space to do her work and cool off. The scene could have turned into a major confrontation if Ida had immediately followed Carole downstairs and marched into the kitchen making comments. Even attempting to work in the same room could easily lead to an argument in a situation like this. When you think there is a good chance your adolescent is going to start making irritable comments, stay out of the way. Remember, *you're not trying to start a fight or get revenge. You are trying to change things* so the problem occurs less frequently in the future.

The threat of an additional chore was an effective way to get Carole to comply with her mother's request to do the dishes. Threats such as this don't work unless the adolescent has learned from past experience that the parent means business and will follow through. Let's take another look at the last scene, this time with the work chore imposed.

Act III: Cleaning the Augean Stables (same cast)

The scene. Ida has asked Carole to do the dishes right now.

Carole: Not now! I'll do the dishes after dinner.

Ida: (in a firm, but neutral voice) Now, Carole, or there

187

will be a work chore as well. The toilet could use a good cleaning.

Carole: (pleading) Mom! Not now!

Ida: (calmly) OK, Carole, now you have to clean the toilet as well. (She immediately turns around and walks downstairs.)

Carole: Well, I'm not going to do it! (Carole shouts down the stairs.) And I'm not going to do the dishes either.

Ida: You'll clean the toilet *and* you'll clean the mirror in the bathroom (Ida says calmly, but loudly enough to be heard as she continues to descend the stairs.) And you will not be able to use the telephone until the toilet, the mirror, and the dishes are done. (With that, Ida walks into her bedroom, closes the door, and takes the phone off the hook. She turns on her own radio, settles into her chair, takes five deep breaths, and picks up her newspaper.)

Commentary

Once again, there were several important things Ida did that insured a successful outcome. In this context, success means that Carole actually completes her chores. The dishes may not get done until after dinner, but the work chores will be finished and so will the dishes before Carole uses the telephone. Take a few minutes and write down what you think Ida did that helped this situation.

Your list should include some of the following: she stayed calm, she imposed the first work chore right away in a neutral tone of voice; she walked away from the scene immediately when Carole started getting angry; she didn't argue, lecture, or offer a rationale; she imposed a second work chore; she stated which privilege would be removed until the chores were completed; she continued to walk down the stairs, and removed herself from the situation by going into her bedroom (this prevented the interaction from escalating), which also helped to calm her down and gave Carole some space to cool down; and finally she took control of the privilege she had removed by taking the telephone off the hook. Now that you have seen how it works, let's go over in detail the steps involved in using five-minute work chores as a disciplinary measure for adolescents.

Eight Steps for Using the Five-Minute Work Chore

1. Set the stage so you will not have to impose a work chore. This is done by creating a friendly atmosphere before making a request. It is also a good idea to time your request (if you can) so that it disrupts things as little as possible. Ida didn't have much choice since she didn't want to cook dinner in a trashed out kitchen.

2. Warn the adolescent that you will impose a work chore as soon as your request is met with noncompliance. If you wait until you are angry, it will be harder for you to do this effectively. In the example above, Ida gave one warning, and only one warning. All too often, parents threaten to use consequences they never intend to impose. Usually this is because the consequence is too extreme. This is one of the advantages of the work chore—it only takes five minutes of work and then things are back to normal again. Keep in mind that your chances of success are better if you act right away.

3. Don't lecture or argue. A discipline encounter is not the time to discuss rationales, intentions, or the rights of adolescents. This may make you feel better, but adolescents are equipped with automatic switches that turn off their ears when there is evidence that a lecture is forthcoming. Arguing also defeats the cooling off principle. It takes two to have an argument, so it is important for you to be strong enough to keep your mouth shut.

189

4. Each time you are about to make a request, have two work chores in mind that you can impose if necessary. You lose bargaining power when the situation arises and you can't think of a chore. "Alright, John, since you won't take the garbage out now, you'll also have to . . . , to . . . , hmmm, you'll have to . . . , hmmmmmm . . ." You can see how this indecisiveness can put you at a disadvantage and diffuse the impact of imposing a chore. Any of the routine household tasks are good, and picking weeds and other types of yard work are also favorites. A list of five-minute work chores that are commonly used by other parents is provided in Appendix 2. Use this list as a starting point, but feel free to add chores that fit your family situation.

5. Impose no more than two work chores before you withdraw a privilege. Once you withdraw the privilege, do not impose any more work chores. Privilege removal signals the end of the discipline confrontation, and you will paint yourself and your adolescent into a corner if you add more chores.

6. Make sure the chore is brief. The chores you assign should be ones that you, or any other person, could complete in five minutes if you were working at a reasonable pace—that's where the "five-minute chore" got its name. Don't get involved in trying to prompt adolescents to hurry up while they are doing the chore. If it takes an hour to scour the kitchen sink, that's their problem. It shouldn't bother you. When the adolescent is finished, check to make sure that a reasonably good job has been done.

7. Stay out of the way while they are doing the work. It is a rare teenager who can accept discipline with a smile. And it is a rare parent who doesn't have the urge to deliver a sarcastic or self-righteous comment about the justice of the work. Hostile interchanges at this point only disrupt the process. Don't tempt yourself—it is almost always better to stay away from the work area as much as you can until the chore is done.

8. Stay calm and neutral. Don't let the quality of your voice match that of your adolescent. You are the parent, and you will be in control if you can avoid losing your temper. You only have to stay cool for a few minutes. If you can do that, you will win in the long run. Winning means teaching your children that there will always be a consequence for noncompliance. Once they understand this, they realize it is easier to comply with your requests than it is to fight them. Think about how pleasant life in your family will be once that lesson is learned. *Whatever you do, stay calm.*

If you or your spouse have trouble controlling the tone of voice used during discipline encounters, set a tape recorder in the kitchen, family room, or other places where the action usually takes place. When a discipline confrontation comes up, turn on the recorder. Play it back for yourself later on in the privacy of your own room. This is one of the homework assignments for Unit 3.

Another trick is to slow your reactions down when you are dealing with an angry confrontation. You'll find that there is an overwhelming tendency to respond reflexively to hostile comments. In the heat of the moment, we all say things that we regret later. Don't let yourself become that ping pong ball bouncing around to someone else's rhythm. Take charge of the exchange by not responding automatically. One trick is the old fashioned technique of silently counting to 10 (or 25 if necessary) before you allow yourself to respond. Another trick is to take three or four really deep breaths. Try to maintain a neutral facial expression while you breathe or count. Your child will not know that you are not reacting to the bait they have offered because you are counting or breathing. Leave the room and go to the bathroom for a minute or two. Pick up the telephone and call the weather report or the time of day recording. Any of these techniques will give you some time to recover your composure. Parents are often surprised to learn how much their own behavior contributes to the intensity of angry confrontations.

Be prepared to remove a privilege if your teenager refuses to do the work. Choosing the proper privilege is extremely important. This is what will induce the teenager to complete the chore without further hassling. The next section will describe how to choose the right privilege.

Privilege Removal: The Back-up Punishment of Choice

When you say, "Do the five-minute work detail or else. . ." that is a threat. How are you going to back it up? The first time they are confronted with a work detail most children refuse to do it, especially if they are angry or convinced that they are the subject of a grave injustice. Our clinical work with severely disrupted families suggests that the withdrawal of a privilege is a great back-up punishment. It is the punishment of choice if the child refuses to do the work detail. This is a good chance for you to teach the adolescent that *you really mean it*, that you will take away television or telephone privileges. These are not inalienable rights guaranteed by the Constitution. They are things that have to be earned, even though most middle class teenagers don't think about it that way. Missing an evening of television or not using the telephone will not "hurt" them a bit, but it will make them think twice about giving you a bunch of back talk.

One of the secrets to success with privilege removal is to take away things that are small, but noticeably important *to the teenager*. Most privileges are taken for granted by teenagers. Make a list of the things that you routinely give to your adolescent. As you make this list, imagine what happens during the day from the moment your teenager wakes up. There's a room, a bed, a home, food in the refrigerator, clothes in the closet, and so on. These are the bare essentials. As you move through a typical day, and a typical week, there are also many *extras*. The extras may include things *you* insist on (piano lessons, haircuts, a certain style of dressing, and so on), as well as things your child demands (rides, car insurance, money, staying at a friend's house, certain clothes that are in style, and so on). On the list of privileges to remove, include things of value to your adolescent but not the bare essentials. Avoid the items that are important to you unless you can stand to withhold them temporarily without guilt or anxiety. Over the next couple of weeks, pay attention to the things you give away, and the things your child tends to take for granted. These are all things that may be candidates for the privilege removal list. This is the first part of the homework assignment for this unit.

Use the same principles with privilege removal that you use with the work chore. Make it brief, make it mild, and make it something you can control. You need to see the disciplinary action through to the end *each and every time*. If you want to change behavior, the best way do it is to win many, small discipline confrontations.

Privilege removals should take place on the day of the incident, because the purpose is to help the child choose the easier way out of the situation, which is to do the work chore. Each discipline confrontation needs to end as quickly as possible. If you ground the child for the week and today is Monday, all week long you will have that disciplinary action hanging over your family like a giant thunderstorm. Extended grounding is not a good disciplinary technique. It is difficult to follow through with it, and it takes a lot of effort on the part of the parent to enforce it (and the child has lots of time to work on you to get out of it).

For adolescents, the most useful privileges to consider are the first three on the following list.

Telephone usage, one day at a time

Television time

Transportation—car use, driving lessons, and rides to and from places

Bicycle, skateboard

Having a friend over

Stereo or radio use

An earlier bedtime or curfew

Grounding, one day at a time

Borrowing things that are taken for granted, for example, clothes, tools, the hair dryer, and so on

Goodies in the refrigerator, for example, ice cream, desserts, and cookies

Each family is different in terms of what privileges really matter, and which ones the parents control. Some families find it impractical to remove television as a privilege because it is centrally located and enjoyed by all family members. In this case, it may be difficult to prevent any one child from watching when the television is on. Another problem with television is that some teenagers don't care about it, so removing the privilege doesn't mean much to them.

Taking away the privilege of telephone use is particularly effective as a back-up punishment for adolescents. It is something that is valued by almost every teenager, and it is relatively easy to control access to the telephone. To remove the privilege, simply unplug the telephones in private areas that are difficult to monitor. This leaves only one telephone, which can be controlled by the parent. Let's say you cannot remove the telephone jack in the adolescent's bedroom, and you catch him or her talking on the phone. Pick up the extension and announce that you are listening. When someone calls in, make sure you answer the telephone. If the call is for your teenager, explain that he or she is unable to talk today, then very politely suggest a return call on the following day.

For younger adolescents, removing bike privileges is often effective. Lock up the bike and carry the key in your pocket. If you have any reason to expect defiance, simply remove the temptation. Take the bike to the home of one of your friends.

If you are removing car privileges, keep all sets of keys with you. There is a chance the adolescent will have a spare key somewhere, so be on the lookout for this. If you are in doubt, check the odometer on any cars that may be used while you are away.

Most adolescents will not leave the house if they are forbidden to do so. If this is true in your family, use grounding *one day at a time*. Never ground children for longer than one day. In our experience, most parents have difficulty monitoring grounding when it lasts longer. If you can't enforce even a one day grounding, use something else that you *can* enforce.

There are other privileges that can be removed which aren't as obvious. Privacy is very important to adolescents, so this is also a candidate. Let's say that Adam is a 16-year-old boy who consistently gets poor grades. His father has been concerned about his performance, and has tried grounding and offering rewards for good grades. But Adam still came home with dismal report cards. This frustrated his father, a professor at the University, who expected his son to do at least reasonably well in school. Adam was certainly bright enough to get "Bs" and "Cs." After thinking about it, Adam's father decided to use a back-up punishment for getting bad grades. He warned Adam that the next time he came home with "Ds" on his report card, he would take the door to Adam's room off the hinges until his grades improved. At first, Adam thought this was funny—big deal, go ahead and take the door away. His report card didn't improve, and his father removed the door. Suddenly, the situation wasn't funny any more. The lack of privacy was devastating to Adam. Everyone could hear him talking on the telephone and singing to the radio. This prompted Adam to work harder on his homework assignments and school projects. His father helped him to develop the components of good study skills (sitting at a desk, making use of the time spent there, and so on). During the next reporting period, Adam's performance was markedly improved. The door was put back on the hinges, and Adam kept his grades at an acceptable level thereafter. Incidentally, this same adolescent is now a young adult, and he has commented that he wished his parents would have pushed him harder in school. This is ironic because Adam resisted every attempt his parents made to get him interested in academics. But this anecdotal account points out the important fact that adolescents don't really know what is best for them in the long run. It is parents who must look after their best interests as they go through this difficult period. Letting your teenager slip too far isn't good, and pulling in the reigns too tightly isn't good either. Parents must find a happy medium in the amount of control they exert over their adolescents.

Setting the Stage for Success

Let your teenager know you will be making some changes. Explain that you are going to be taking responses to your requests very seriously from now on. This means that each time you make a request the teenager will either receive points for cooperating or a five-minute work chore for being disobedient. Disobedience means not doing as asked within 15 seconds. Explain to the teenager that these changes will make your life easier as a parent because it will reduce the back talk and arguing, and that the teenager will also benefit from the changes because it will cut down on your nagging. Don't just point the finger at the adolescent, take some responsibility for your contribution to the problem of not getting along. The new program is also an opportunity for the teenager to earn additional privileges with the points you are providing for compliance. It also means that things will be more predictable in terms of car use and so on. If your youngster earns the privilege, then you can't take it away or say no because you are in a bad mood.

Describe the procedure you will be using. The rules are as follows: 1) when you make a request you expect compliance within 15 seconds; 2) if the teenager doesn't comply with the request within the specified time you will label the lack of response as not minding, and a warning will be given that a work chore will be forthcoming without immediate compliance; 3) failure to comply means the work chore will be assigned; 4) after assigning a work chore, walk away from the scene to give your youngster some space; 5) if the adolescent continues to ignore the original request, then give a warning that one more work chore will be assigned if compliance doesn't follow immediately; 6) further noncompliance and/or refusal to carry out these chores will result in the removal of a privilege until the chores are completed. Explain that arguing is not going to change things. If the child would like to discuss the situation, it can be done at another time, after the work chore is complete and both parties are calm. Don't expect your teenager to welcome this new arrangement.

Here's how Ida first explained the ground rules for the work chore to Carole.

Act IV: Some Changes Are Forthcoming
(same cast)

The Scene. Ida and Carole have just finished dinner. A friendly atmosphere prevails. It's Thursday and both of them have plans for the weekend. Ida hates to break the pleasantness of the evening by discussing something that is bound to get Carole upset, but she also knows that it is better to discuss the new program now so she can start using it.

Ida: Carole, there's something I'd like to talk to you about.

Carole: Uh oh, what's the matter now?

Ida: Well, I've been thinking about all the arguments we seem to have, and I'm going to do something different from now on to change that.

Carole: Great! You're gonna quit bugging me, right?

Ida: Actually, I am. From now on when I ask you to do something I'll continue to give you a point for minding, but when you don't do as I ask there will be a consequence. You'll have to do a five-minute work chore when you don't mind me.

Carole: What do you think I am, some sort of robot?

Ida: (calmly continuing) A five-minute work chore means just that. If you don't do as I ask, you will end up doing a short chore. If you argue or refuse, then I will have to assign another chore. At that point, if you don't do both chores, you will lose a privilege like use of the telephone until you complete the chores. Do you have any questions?

Carole: Where did you get that stupid idea—from one of those television psychologists like Dr. Ruth?

Ida: It doesn't matter. Do you have any questions about how this works?

Carole: (leaving the table in a huff) I don't care what you say, I'm not doing a bunch of chores for you. Do them yourself!

Ida: Well, this is just a warning. Things are going to be different around here from now on. Not minding my requests will result in a five-minute work chore. If you do it right away, you will get points for minding. If you don't, you'll end up doing some additional chores and maybe even lose a privilege for the rest of the day. It doesn't have to be a negative thing—if you simply do what I ask then you will get points for extra privileges like use of the car or extra telephone time. I'm going to do my part by making fewer requests, and by timing my requests so that they don't interfere with something you are doing. You'll end up with less nagging from me and we won't have to keep arguing about little stuff all the time. This is something that is supposed to work for both of us. I just want us to get along. (She gets up and goes calmly into her room.)

Teenagers will say just about anything they can to save face or throw you off course when you tell them that you are changing the rules. Don't pay attention to what they say, and don't get caught up in defending what you are doing. Above all, don't act angry, argumentative or vindictive. Try to be as dispassionate as possible, as though you are simply describing the rules of a new game that is meant for the whole family. It is typical for teenagers to be angry or hostile at this point, so ignore it. There is no reason to let the issue become emotionally charged. Simply state the rules and calmly go about your business. During the next few days both you and your adolescent will have plenty of opportunities to practice imposing and performing five-minute work chores.

One more hint. The first few times you try it, things may not go smoothly. You are bound to make some mistakes. Just like any other skill, it will take practice to master this one. After you have had several discipline encounters, reread this chapter to pick up the points you missed the first time through.

Key Ideas in this Chapter (Unit Two)

1. The five-minute work chore is an effective punishment.
2. Use a consequence for back talk.
3. There are eight steps for using the five-minute work chore: 1) create a friendly atmosphere; 2) make it clear that noncompliance means doing a work chore; 3) don't lecture or provide a rationale; 4) have at least two work chores in mind; 5) after two chores have been imposed, remove a privilege for further noncompliance; 6) select short work chores; 7) stay away while the work is in progress; and 8) stay as neutral as possible.
4. Use privilege removal as a back-up punishment. Have a list of privileges to remove at your disposal before you have a discipline encounter with your adolescent.

Chapter Six (Unit Two) Homework Assignment

There are three parts to the homework assignment for this unit. These assignments are intended to prepare you for discipline encounters with your adolescent, so spend some time working on this and be thorough. Your efforts here will enhance your chances of success. The first homework assignment is to come up with a list of privileges to remove. Look over the list we have provided at the end of this unit, and think creatively about the things your adolescent values or enjoys. For the next week or so take notes on the privileges your adolescent tends to take for granted. After you have generated a list of a dozen or more candidates, assign priorities to them. Think carefully about the privileges at the top of the list. How can you control access to them?

List of Privileges to Remove

	Description	Priority
1.		
2.		
3.		
4.		
5.		
6.		
7.		
8.		
9.		
10.		
11.		
12.		
13.		
14.		
15.		

Next, tell your adolescent what to expect. Don't use this as an opportunity to lecture. Simply state that from now on noncompliance will mean doing a short work chore. Arguing about it will mean doing another work chore. Furthermore, a privilege (such as telephone use) will be removed until the two chores are completed. Then leave the room—you don't want to get into an argument at this point.

The third part of the assignment is to follow through with imposing a work chore *every time* your adolescent is noncompliant.

Discipline
Unit 3

Using Longer Work Chores for More
Serious Problems

During the course of everyday events, it is natural for adolescents to test their limits and yours as well. This means that as a parent you will need consequences that are appropriate for a wide variety of problems, some of which are more serious than others. We have found that work details are surprisingly flexible in this regard. Serious infractions may involve work chores longer than five minutes. Skipping a class at school, for example, might result in an hour of weed picking, but a police offense such as shoplifting might require several hours of work on the woodpile. It is important to negotiate the consequences in advance for common problems. For unexpected problems, give yourself some time to think of an appropriate consequence. The drama that follows illustrates how to use more extensive work details as a consequence for bigger problems.

Act I: The Midnight Rider (Stan & Ruth)

One of the most common problems teenagers have is meeting their time commitments. Work details are a perfect contingency for this problem. Most teenagers have good intentions when it comes to being on time, but when they are enjoying themselves, they often "forget" to check the clock. They often have legitimate excuses for being late, but that doesn't change things for you as a parent when you are worried about them, or waiting for them to come home for dinner. Once again, it is important to remember that your goal is to teach your teenager to be on time by using consequences for lateness. Let's take a look at a family managing this problem with work as the consequence.

The Scene. Ruth and Stan have three children: Mike, 16; Patti, 14; and George, 12. It's almost midnight, and Ruth and Stan are sitting in front of the television watching the Johnny Carson Show.

Ruth: (She gets up and goes into the kitchen to look at the clock on the stove. Returning to her place on the couch, she puts her hand on her husband's knee.) I'm worried. Mike has never been this late before. He said he'd be home by 10:30. Where could he be?

Stan: Come on, Ruth. Relax. He's just late, I'm sure that everything is O.K.

Ruth: He's never this late. Something must have happened. I think I should call Lynda's mother and find out if he's over there, or if she's heard from the kids.

Stan: What time is it now?

Ruth: Almost 12 o'clock.

Stan: Well, that's the last time Mike gets to borrow the car for awhile.

Ruth: What should we do? Should I call Lynda's mother? Should I call the police? He must have had an accident or something.

Stan: Where is he supposed to be?

Ruth: At the library, but I know it's closed now. It closed at 10 o'clock. I thought I was being more than reasonable by letting him stay out until 10:30.

Stan: Well, let's wait until midnight and then call the police station to see if there have been any accidents. I don't think we should let him go out on school nights anyway.

Ruth: But he said he had this important project that was due and absolutely HAD to use the library to finish it.

Stan: (sarcastically) I'll *bet* he went to the library. Don't you remember using that excuse when we were in high school? Someone's parents are probably out of town, and he and Lynda are over there partying it up right now.

Ruth: Well, but sometimes the library is a legitimate place to go, and it isn't always possible to check on him.

Stan: Maybe we better start trying to do more of that. This isn't the first time he's been late on a school night.

Ruth: But he's never been *this* late before. It's always been less than an hour. I'm so worried. (She sniffles and her eyes fill with tears.)

Stan: (putting his arm around her and giving her a gentle squeeze) Come on, honey. He's alright. He's just late. He's probably off in some dark lane necking with Lynda.

The sound of a car pulling into the driveway interrupts their conversation. Ruth goes into the kitchen to take another look at the clock. It's three minutes past 12. Instead of looking relieved, her face is drawn into an angry scowl. She puts her hands on her hips and stands at the back door. Stan gazes at the television, letting his wife take the lead in this scene. The boy walks in the door with an innocent expression on his face, and hugs his mother.

Mike: Hi, Mom. Sorry I'm late. Did you worry?

Ruth: Did I worry? What a question! What do you think I've been doing? Do you realize what time it is?

Mike: (apologetically) I know, I know. I'm sorry. Don't you want to know what happened?

Ruth: Do I want to know what happened, he asks me! Don't you think I want to know where my 16-year-old son has been in my car until midnight on a school night?

Mike: Hey, Mom. Calm down. It's not my fault I'm late. You don't need to get so hysterical about this.

Stan: (speaking up from his spot on the couch in front of the television) You just watch yourself, young man. YOU are the one in trouble, not your mother. WHERE HAVE YOU BEEN?

Mike: (looking down at the floor) Well, I don't suppose you are going to believe this, but I had a flat tire.

Stan: (his face showing his disbelief) Come on Mike—you can do better than that. Do you really expect us to believe a lame excuse like that?

Mike: (a bit more aggressively) Well, I knew you weren't going to believe me. You guys never believe me. There's no use even trying to talk to you. (He starts to walk toward his room, throwing his keys across the kitchen counter.)

Stan: You come over here and sit down! No! First, you go back in the kitchen and put those goddamned keys on the hook where they belong. *Then* you come in here and sit down.

Ruth walks into the family room and sits on the couch beside her husband. Mike does as he's told. Then, he slowly walks over to the chair farthest from the couch and sits

206

down. He cups his chin in his hands, and looks blankly toward the television.

Stan: (He gets up and turns off the television, then addresses Mike in a firm, no nonsense voice.) Alright, where have you been?

Mike: (in a condescending tone of voice, like he is talking to someone who is extremely ignorant) I've been at the library working on my science project just like I said I was.

Stan: (maintaining a calm tone of voice and looking directly at him) The library closes at 10:30.

Ruth: (interrupting briefly) No, it closes at 10 o'clock.

Stan: Whatever the time. It's *midnight* now. Where the hell have you been from 10 o'clock until now? The library is only two miles from here. You could have *walked* from here to there several times in two hours.

Mike: I *told* you. I had a flat tire.

Stan: (anger is beginning to show on his face) Don't hand me that cock and bull story. . . .

Ruth: (interrupting) And besides, it doesn't take two hours to change a flat tire. I can change a tire in 15 minutes myself. You'd think a clever boy like you could do it at least as well as I can.

Mike: (deftly sidetracking the issue by bringing up a minor detail) I'm only an hour and-a-half late, not two hours. You guys always exaggerate things.

Stan: Cut the crap and go to bed! Your mother and I will discuss this and let you know what the consequence will be in the morning.

Mike: Don't I get a chance to explain?

Stan: Not now. It's late, and your mother and I are too angry to want to talk about it any more. We'll talk about it tomorrow. Now go to bed!

Mike: (walking out of the room, shaking his head, and muttering to himself just loud enough to be heard) I can't believe it, *I* have a lousy flat tire, and now my ass is in a sling. . . . What a great night.

Commentary

Most teenagers have to *learn* to be on time, even if they have been relatively prompt as younger children. There are just too many temptations and new situations for adolescents to cope with for them to always be responsible about their time commitments. Focus on teaching them to be on time. If you are using a point chart, you will want to include being on time as behavior that earns points. In any case, when you are raising an adolescent you will want to anticipate this problem and have some good back-up consequences for being late.

Notice how well Ruth and Stan worked together in the scene above to handle this difficult situation. Before the boy came home, the father was warm and comforting to his worried wife. Parents do tend to worry about the safety of their children. This is a good quality for parents to have, as long as it's not carried to extremes. When the boy finally came home, the father supported the mother's position when Mike started talking back to her. If, on the other hand, Stan had let that little comment about getting hysterical pass, then it is very likely that Mike would have escalated the intensity of his attack. Even though Mike was right that his mother was not being perfectly calm and rational, she had good reason to be upset. When there are two parents in the family, it is very helpful if the parent who is least angry acts as the moderator for both the child and the other parent. It is easy to get emotionally charged when you are dealing with adolescents, and it is important to learn some techniques for cooling down the situation. Stan and Ruth did that by ending the confrontation with Mike as soon as it was clear that they could not have a rational discussion.

Let's see how this family resolved the situation.

Act II: The Midnight Rider
(same cast, a few minutes later)

Stan: Do you want to talk about this now, or do you want to wait until tomorrow?

Ruth: The way I feel now, I'll never be able to go to sleep.

Stan: OK, then let's talk about it.

Ruth: (She goes to the refrigerator and gets them both a beer.) So he was an hour and-a-half late. You mentioned not letting him use the car for awhile. How long do you think we should wait until we let him use the car again?

Stan: If we removed his car privileges for a week or two, maybe he would think twice about pulling that stunt again.

Ruth: Yeah, but how long do you think we'd stick to it, really? A day, two days, a week?

Stan: Well, we haven't been very successful at staying with it in the past. Two weeks is a long time to hide the keys, check the odometer, and all that stuff. And besides, if he can't use the car then we have to run him around to his lessons, and that's a hassle for us. Here's an idea—what if we make him work it off? Maybe we should do something like make him work a minute or two for every minute he was late. Let's see. That would be 90 minutes of work. Do we have that much work around here for him to do?

Ruth: I like that! We could do it just like the five-minute work chore, only it would be longer. It's October, and there are leaves that need raking. How can we set it up so that neither of us has to stand over him to make sure he's working the whole time? I don't

209

want to be anywhere near him when he's got a punishment detail.

Stan: The front yard is pretty big. Don't you think that's about an hour and-a-half's worth of work, that is, for someone working at a steady pace?

Ruth: I guess so, especially if he has to pile them next to the curb for pick up. But how will we get him to do it? What if he refuses?

Stan: We'll take away his privileges until he finishes the chore—no telephone, no car, no going out, no nothing. It'll cost him if he wants to be obstinate.

Ruth: OK, that's good. Let's do it! I'll write this down.

Act III: The Summit Meeting (same cast, next day)

The Scene. The activity level in the house is fairly hectic. The two younger children are rushing around getting ready for school. Both parents are preparing to leave for work. Mike is the only person looking lethargic. He sits at the dining room table, scowling and slowly crunching his cereal. Ruth comes into the kitchen to pour herself another cup of coffee and looks over in his direction.

Ruth: Your father and I have decided what your consequence will be. Do you want to discuss it now, or wait until this evening?

Mike: I don't care. Do as you like.

Ruth: OK. We'll discuss it tonight.

(That evening, Mom, Dad, and Mike sit down and discuss the consequence before dinner. The atmosphere is fairly calm.)

Mike: So I have to rake the whole front yard? That'll take more than an hour and-a-half!

Stan: Maybe so. Both your mother and I decided we could do it that fast. Take your time, but make sure you do

210

it right. You have no privileges until it's done—no telephone, no car, no going out. When you think you are done, tell either your mother or me and we'll take a look at it.

Ruth: And we also decided that we will use work as a consequence for being late in the future. Before midnight, it will cost you a minute of work for a minute of being late. If, however, you come home later than midnight, it will cost you double time on chores. That's because we worry more after midnight.

Mike: What I want to know is, how long am I grounded?

Ruth: You aren't grounded. You will be able to use the car, and all of the other privileges will be reinstated as soon as you finish your work. You have no privileges until your work is done.

Mike: It's all the same thing. You're telling me I'm grounded.

Ruth: If you want to think about it that way, then I guess you're right. You are grounded, but only until you finish your work and it passes inspection. You can take as much time, or as little time, as you like. You could be done in an hour and a half from right now, if you went right out there and raked the leaves.

The telephone rings, and it is a call for Mike. Patti answers the telephone and yells, "It's for you, Mike." Mike moves toward the telephone.

Stan: Not now, Mike. When you finish raking the leaves, you may answer the telephone.

Mike: But that's ridiculous. It might be something important.

Stan: Well, it will have to wait. (to his daughter) Tell whoever it is that Mike can't talk right now. He'll have to call back when he's finished his work.

211

Guidelines for Using Longer Chores

The principles involved in using lengthy chores for larger transgressions are similar to the ones we have discussed for the five-minute chore. The following are some suggestions.

1. Make it mild (it is NOT revenge). You want the punishment to be mild, but you also want it to fit the crime. Use short punishments for small problems, and longer punishments for bigger problems. The parents in the example above decided that being late after midnight was more of a problem than being late before midnight, so they added the

Jennifer's Night Out

Remember to be home by midnight, Cinderella, or you'll be working in the yard tomorrow...

"double time" rule to distinguish between the two types of lateness.

Before you decide to use a new consequence, think it through carefully in advance. For example, if you say there will be 10 minutes of work for every minute the teenager is late, and your adolescent is three hours late, you would have to supervise 30 hours of work. Most parents would be unable, or unwilling, to follow through on a consequence such as this. It is better to use a mild punishment that is easier for you to monitor (it is also doubtful that 30 hours of work would be more effective in changing behavior than a 90-minute chore).

The age of your child is one of the factors that should be considered when you are assigning consequences for problem behaviors. For a younger adolescent you might use two minutes of work for every minute the child is late after 8 p.m. because you worry. School nights might be different from weekend nights. Extended work chores can work well for a multitude of teenage sins. Some examples of crimes and appropriate punishments are provided below.

The Crime	The Punishment
Lying	30 minutes (15 minutes if you strongly *suspect* but are somewhat uncertain).
Truancy	For missing a single class, one minute of work for one minute of class missed. For missing a whole day, four or five hours of work.
Noncompliance	A five-minute work chore.
Smoking	One hour for each time caught (if only suspected, you might make it 15 or 20 minutes).
A call from school or neighbor because of rowdy behavior	30 minutes to one hour depending on seriousness.
Staying out all night	One full day's work.

213

Remember, it's not an eye for an eye or a tooth for a tooth that is involved here. You are just trying to teach the child to stop doing something specific like coming home late. Don't give up on a mild punishment because it doesn't eliminate the problem behavior the first few times you use it. It may take several discipline encounters before your adolescent understands that you mean business.

Don't change the rules in midstream. You may need to change the rules you set up initially, but give a warning first. And if you do make changes, continue to impose punishments that are mild enough to use *each and every time* the problem comes up.

You can, on rare occasions, lighten punishments that are almost impossible to see through to the bitter end. But when you do this, you lose a bit of dignity and a small part of the war. If, in a moment of passion, you ground your adolescent for a month, and then decide it is too difficult to follow through (or that it is not reasonable to follow through) there is a way to back out of it and save face. This involves trading grounding time for some important effort put forth by the adolescent. For example, if you grounded your teenager for two months, you could subtract time for good behavior *and* for one hour of work reduce the sentence by one week. If you do this, make sure that all eight hours of work are completed to your satisfaction before restoring privileges. The important thing is to require adolescents to *earn* back the privileges removed. If you don't follow through with some sort of consequence, it teaches the adolescent that you don't mean what you say (your punishments become "threats" instead of a meaningful consequence). The best policy is to choose an appropriate and *MILD* punishment in the first place, one that you will carry out without alteration.

2. Make it clear. It is important to describe chores in detail so that there is no room for confusion and debate. In the example above, the chore was not well defined. Exactly what do Ruth and Stan want done? Where are the boundaries of the front yard? Do they want Mike to rake the leaves trapped in and around the edges of shrubs and bushes? Perhaps Mike has done this job before and knows what is expected, but it wouldn't hurt to provide a detailed description of what the job entails. It is a good idea to list your expectations for the job on paper. Be as specific as possible. Outline what you want done as if a stranger were going to do the work.

3. **If you must remove a privilege.** Let's say that the work detail is not getting done. At this point you want to make sure that you follow through and back up your threat to remove privileges. If you remove a privilege such as telephone use it is important to monitor whether or not the child has access to the telephone. If you don't do a good job of monitoring, the consequence will have little or no effect. Make sure you remove privileges that are not too difficult to monitor.

It is also a good idea to establish the length of time for which privileges will be removed. In the previous example, Mike would lose all privileges for a week if he refuses to do the work chore. This may mean that Mike gets to use the car at the end of the week even though the yard has not been raked (although this is unlikely—most teenagers can't survive without a car for that long). If it works out that way, that's all right. The loss of privileges was, by itself, a good consequence for staying out late. You don't have to win on all counts to change behavior. The important thing is to make sure that problem behaviors result in a specific negative consequence for the adolescent.

4. **Provide personal space while the work is in progress.** If you can't leave the house, find something to do that will remove you from the area where the work detail is being done. Most teenagers tend to ask a lot of questions, make comments, or in some other way try to involve you in the

process of doing the work. Once the chore is clearly understood (ask the adolescent if there are any questions after the chore is explained in detail), then the time for discussion is over. Don't interrupt your teenager while the chore is in progress.

If you notice that your teenager is doing the work, but is slamming things around or showing contempt in other ways, ignore the behavior unless you feel that something or someone is likely to be damaged. Teenagers have a lot of energy, and in many cases they need to blow off a little steam. This is also a good way to get some attention for negative behavior (which reinforces the behavior). If you decide you *must* intervene because it appears that something may be broken, calmly announce that anything that is damaged will have to be repaired or replaced before privileges are reinstated, then leave. If you are absent while they do the chore (at least for the first 30 minutes or so), it helps to insulate you from angry reactions. Go to the store and pick up some groceries, find a good book and read it in your bedroom, or watch the news while they do the chore. Some parents wear headphones and listen to music to block out the noise. The main idea is to make sure that you are not involved while they are doing the work.

Sometimes the offending teenager will mistreat your other children while at work. The best approach is to tell the siblings to stay away. It is very difficult (and not particularly worthwhile) to make the adolescent be cheerful while doing the chore. If the siblings continue to hang around, give *them* a five-minute chore for disobedience. If they were really "innocent bystanders," they would not have been within range after you told them to stay away.

Avoid making sarcastic comments, using "put downs," or poking fun at the teenager in this situation. Adolescents have a right to be treated with respect even when they are in trouble.

5. Inspect the work site. This, too, must be done in a neutral style. If your teenager has done a rotten job, simply restate your expectations. Here's where writing down the components of the chore comes in handy. If your child becomes angry, star the items on the list that must be completed, and *walk away*. Be calm; don't argue. Remember who is the adult. If the youngster tears up the list, walk away and write another one. Later on, when the worker decides to continue the job so privileges can be restored, you can simply hand over the new list.

6. When the consequence is finished, drop the topic. Some parents demand an admission of guilt or some other final response from their adolescent when the work is done. There is something satisfying about that, like a piece of pumpkin pie after Thanksgiving dinner. But don't do it. Don't ask them to tell you *why* they had to do the work. Don't ask them if they learned their lesson.

When the job is done, make some positive comments about the work and erase the incident from your mind. Adolescents usually remember these discipline encounters better than parents do, although it is unlikely that they will mention it to their parents again. They will describe the sequence of events to their friends, and someday, when they are parents, they will probably use the same consequences with their own children.

For Really Long Work Chores

Some offenses are so big (like shoplifting, or drinking while driving) they require a heavier consequence, that is, a job that cannot be completed in a single day. In this case, you need to set up the chore so that a certain amount of work must be completed each day. A good strategy is to tell the child that privileges will be restored *for the day* after a certain amount of work is finished.

How much work time should be required each day? An

hour or two is usually all that an adolescent can manage given other responsibilities like homework, a part-time job outside the home, or other important commitments. It is not necessary to make a big deal out of this by interrupting the normal schedule to accommodate the work detail. During weekends, five or six hours is reasonable for older adolescents. But require at least one hour of work each day so it is difficult for the teenager to "forget" about the work that needs to be done.

Can Work Chores Create Problems?

Some parents don't like to use work chores as a punishment for bad behavior. They may worry, for example, that this might teach children to hate working. Some types of work, by their very nature, are unpleasant. Other types of work are more satisfying. The best types of work to use for punishment are boring and/or unpleasant jobs that never get done because nobody volunteers for them. All of our children had to deal with one or more rounds of work details while they were teenagers, and yet none of them seems to hate working as an adult. It is relatively easy for adolescents to distinguish between work that is required as a punishment and working to earn money.

Fines

Using fines is an effective alternative to using work chores for punishment. Money is very meaningful to adolescents, and losing it is a powerful consequence for them. Charging a fine for problem behaviors satisfies all of the requirements for a good punishment. To illustrate how to use fines as a punishment, let's use tardiness as the problem behavior. A good approach would be to charge a certain amount of money for every minute the adolescent is late. The following are some guidelines for using fines for lateness.

1. Base the amount charged on your child's economic situation. If your child has a lot of money, the fines should be large. If money is tight, the fines should be smaller. A fine of $.05 for every minute late adds up to $3 per hour. A double charge after midnight (or some other preestablished time) would cost $6 per hour. Remember to keep the punishment *mild* enough to be able to use it *every time* the problem behavior occurs.

2. Remove privileges until the fine is paid. Follow the same guidelines for privilege removal that were given for longer work chores. Remove only those privileges you are certain you can control.

3. What to do when the culprit is "broke." Offer the adolescent an opportunity to earn money immediately by doing work for you. Follow the guidelines given for using work as a punishment, including defining the job, staying out of the way, checking on the finished job, and so on. Do not reinstate the adolescent's privileges until the work is done and the fine is paid. Do *not* allow the teenager to owe you money for a fine.

The "Nap"

There are many consequences that can be used in addition to the ones we have described here. Punishments need to fit the situation and the age of the child. Time Out, for example, is an excellent way to stop younger children (ages two through 12) from engaging in problem behaviors. The basic approach used in the Time Out technique is to isolate the child in an uninteresting place for a few minutes. This stops the ongoing behavior, such as teasing, and gives the child some time to cool off. By removing the child from the room, it also prevents the child from arguing or getting further attention for bad behavior. The procedure is fully described in *Families*, a book by Gerald Patterson that focuses on managing the behavior of younger children (a videotape entitled Time Out! is also available from OSLC).

Our colleague, Dr. Patricia Chamberlain, has found a way to modify the Time Out procedure so it can be used with adolescents. She recommends using the modified Time Out technique as a punishment for that all-too-common problem of adolescent "bad attitude." Bad attitude is a malaise that creeps up on youngsters just as they slip into their adolescent years. It begins when children discover that their parents are not perfect, and their peers are. With this realization, they gradually develop a holier-than-thou approach to dealing with parents that becomes almost palpable. The symptoms of this malaise are withdrawal from family life to the safety of their bedrooms, and long hot showers. Parents might also begin to notice the emergence of a subtle (or sometimes not so subtle) irritability. Most parents find this change disconcerting and don't know how to cope with it. Patti's technique is called the "NAP." Here's how it works.

In order to use the nap properly, parents must be able to understand the difficulties faced by adolescents. Teenagers *are* under a great deal of stress. During their day-by-day experiences they are confronted by many new situations, and they don't have the necessary skills to deal with them, yet they feel compelled to act as if they know all the answers. Their bodies are changing rapidly. Their complexions become a horror that confronts them every time they stand in front of a mirror. Hormones may also take them through startling mood swings. They attempt to relate to members of the opposite sex, but don't quite understand the rules of this new game. It's no wonder that they become surly and a little irritable. Even though you sympathize with their problems, you don't want their bad attitude to pollute the environment of your happy home. How do you deal with it? The answer is that you listen to their problems, but when they begin to show signs that a bad attitude is building, you send them to their room for a nap.

Here's a scene between Mike and his dad that demonstrates how to use the nap.

Mike Takes a Nap

The Scene. It's Saturday morning and Mike has just made an appearance after spending two hours behind the closed door of his bedroom. He's been working out with his weights, and is covered with sweat. He heads to the bathroom for a shower, but it is occupied by this sister who is blow drying her hair.

Mike: (knocking loudly on the door) Hey! Hurry up in there!

Patti: Buzz off!

Mike: (now pounding on the door) Come on! It's my turn in there. You might as well give up on the beauty treatment anyway. You're a hopeless case.

Patti ignores him. The hair dryer continues to drone behind the bathroom door, and now it is accompanied by Patti singing in the background. Mike begins pounding on the door with one hand and rattling the doorknob with the other.

Dad: Hey, Mike. Leave her alone.

Mike stops his attack on the bathroom door, walks into the family room, and sits down in front of the TV where a football game is playing. His face looks like a thunderstorm that is just about to explode.

Dad: Are you in a hurry?

Mike: I just wanted to take a shower. I'm all sweaty, and she's been in there all day. How long do I have to wait for the fairy princess to emerge from her chamber?

Dad: (pleasantly) Let's give her another 10 minutes. Then the bathroom's yours.

Mike: TEN MINUTES! You must be kidding! I have to wait 10 MINUTES for that . . . that ugly, selfish, little slob to finish her so-called beauty treatment! You *always* take her side! How come you *never* see things my way?

Dad: Hey. Slow down kiddo. You're getting yourself all worked up over this. In a family like this with only one bathroom, sometimes you have to wait. I think you're just tired from your workout. Why don't you go back in your room for 10 minutes and take a rest while she finishes up. I'll call you when it's time for her to come out.

The Wrong Way

It would be easy to turn this scene into a disaster. All it would take to start an argument is a single angry response from the dad. An argument could easily escalate into a battle that could ruin the whole weekend.

(When Mike sits down, his father looks over at him.)

Dad: (in an irritable and self righteous tone) Why do you pick on her like that? She has a right to the bathroom too, you know. Just wait your turn like everyone else.

Mike: Oh, you *always* take her side. We all know how you play favorites with the fairy princess.

Dad: (With a rising inflection in his voice and a scowl on his face, he leans toward his son.) You better watch yourself, young man! I'm sick and tired of having to deal with you and your surly attitude. You could stand to learn a little. . . .

Mike gets up and slams the door on the way into his bedroom. A few minutes later he storms out of the house, and he's gone for the rest of the afternoon. This outcome is upsetting to Stan and Ruth—Stan is angry because he feels that he was in the right, but somehow he lost the confrontation anyway; Ruth is distraught because she knows Mike will receive a large consequence for taking off without telling them where he was going, and that there may be an additional confrontation with Mike during the weekend as a result of all this. Tonight there is a big party at Lynda's house, and Mike had been planning to go for weeks. A good consequence would be to tell Mike that he can't go to the party because of the way he was acting this morning, but this would have repercussions for the next two weeks, at least. Now it seems like there is no simple solution to the problem, and the unfortunate thing is that it all started over something so insignificant. Perhaps they should have told Patti to let him use the bathroom. . . .

Mike doesn't even know what happened to him. He just wanted to take a shower and because his sister, who has always been a bathroom hog, wouldn't let him use it, he got into an unpleasant confrontation with his father. None of this was planned. Why do these things keep happening to him, he wonders. What can he do now? There is a knot in his stomach because he knows that there's going to be hell to pay when he gets home. . . .

The best approach for the parents would have been to avoid the situation in the first place. Suppose you attempt to use the nap as a technique for dealing with a surly attitude, and your teenager refuses to go. Then it's time to add a work chore. Here's how that could have been done.

Dad: Mike, you seem all worked up right now. Why don't you go into your room and rest for a few minutes. Before you know it, Patti will be out of there and you'll have your hot shower.

Mike: I'm *not* worked up. She's got no right to stay in there all day. (He gets up and goes back to the bathroom door and pounds on it again.)

Dad: (Getting out of his chair, he gives Mike full eye contact without looking threatening.) Mike, I told you to wait. Either go in your room and take a rest right now, or go outside and sweep the sidewalk. It's your choice.

Mike's whole face tightens into a scowl. He briefly glares at his father, looks at the bathroom door, and clenches his fists. Then he turns, strides down the hall and closes his bedroom door firmly (almost slamming it, but not quite). His father shakes his head, and mutters under his breath about the difficulty of living with teenagers.

Commentary

The main point here is to give the adolescent a choice (the Mafia calls this "making an offer he can't refuse"). This gives the boy some room to move. He has clearly crossed the line. But his show of bad attitude, while it is a major problem in that it can lead to bigger conflicts, can be controlled with a minor consequence like the nap. If the adolescent refuses to comply with the suggestion to rest for a few minutes, then the parent is forced to escalate the intensity of the consequence by adding the work chore. Further disobedience will result in loss of privileges, which Mike wants to avoid at all costs because Lynda's party is coming up.

But this technique cannot work unless the parent is adult enough to refrain from responding in kind to irritable behavior. The parent needs to stay calm, even be understanding, but firm, in suggesting a "nap."

Key Ideas in this Chapter (Unit Three)

1. Make sure you discuss the behavior change program with your adolescent. We have said this several times before, but it is very important—the way in which you present it will make a big difference in the way it is received. Re-

member, your adolescent has to be willing to comply with the changes you are putting into motion.

2. In summary, good punishments have the following characteristics:
   1. They are mild.
   2. They are over quickly.
   3. They can be used every time the problem behavior occurs.
   4. Their effect is to weaken and stop problem behaviors.
   5. They work best when used with a system of positive reinforcement for good behavior.

Chapter Six (Unit Three) Homework Assignment

1. Before you try using longer work chores or the "nap" practice it with your partner or a friend first. Ask your friend to play the part of your child and you try to manage a typical "bad attitude" situation using the "nap." Try it at least twice. The first time through, get surly and irritable yourself and notice the outcome. The next time try to stay calm and in control. Pretend you're on TV so you can be the rational parent you'd like to be. Remember, anger, sarcasm, and hostility just accelerate the intensity of the exchange without changing behavior.

Another way to try this out is to have your partner or friend play the part of the parent, and you play the part of your adolescent. Do it both ways again so that you can experience how it feels to be on the receiving end of a confrontation with a parent in control versus a parent out of control.

If you don't want to practice this with another person present, try to "dry run" the situation in your head. Imagine a typical confrontation with your adolescent. Put yourself in the driver's seat the first time by staying calm, and visualize your child choosing to "take a nap." Then go through the scene again and visualize what it feels like to let yourself lose control and become a ping pong ball bouncing off your child's paddle. Imagine the argument that would follow. Then go through the scene with yourself in charge one more time. It really helps to plan these confrontations in advance, and, as the old saying goes, "practice makes perfect."

One more way to help yourself manage these situations is to tape record discipline encounters and play them back in the privacy of your own room. When you are in the midst of a fight, you are not in control, and you are not fully aware of what you are doing or what your child is doing.

2. Begin using longer work chores for more serious adolescent problems. Try using the "nap" for mild problems.

Chapter Six References

1. The studies on punishment are reviewed in Chapter 6 in Patterson, G. R. *Coercive Family Process*. Eugene, OR: Castalia Publishing Company, 1982.

2. Paul, Gordon L., and Lentz, R. J. "Psychosocial Treatment of Chronic Mental Patients: A Review by Sandra Loucks." *Contemporary Psychology*, 1978, 23, 642-644.

3. White, G. D., Nielsen, G., and Johnson, S. M. "Time Out Duration and the Suppression of Deviant Behavior in Children." *Journal of Applied Behavior Analysis*, 1972, 5, 111-120.

CHAPTER 7

Family Processes— Slow Changes, Dramatic Outcomes Unit 1

How is it that well-intentioned parents end up raising problem children? Many of the parents we see at our research center find themselves asking this question. Our current understanding of families does provide some answers, but they are not simple ones. We believe families change so slowly that the people involved in them do not notice what is going on. These changes are the result of *processes* that operate within families. A husband who becomes distant and uninvolved, a depressed mother, and a teenager who is acting out all have something in common. The problems they are experiencing are the result of disruptive family processes.

There are many *small* changes in family living taking place day by day that tend to slip by unnoticed. These are small changes in how we feel and little shifts in patterns of thought and social interaction. These changes reflect the kinds of experiences we have had in the recent past. In most cases these changes don't go anywhere. But in other cases, these tiny shifts signal the beginning of processes that can lead to massive changes in family life. So far, most of our studies have focused on the processes that disrupt families. We also know, however, that other processes promote growth in positive directions. The purpose of this chapter is to help parents understand how processes which are composed of many small events can produce dramatic changes in their families.

A Definition of Process

The general meaning of the term "process" is a series of changes or actions that build upon one another to bring about an end result. Before we discuss how this relates to families, we will illustrate the concept in more general terms.

A process that we are all familiar with is the aging process. Even during adolescence, when children are growing rapidly, we fail to notice the many small changes in appearance that take place day by day. After these changes build on one another for a few months, the result becomes more obvious. Then you may notice that your adolescent son can't get his shoes on, and his pants are too short. When you pull out the family picture album, the changes seem even more dramatic. Now you can see that your little boy is growing into a young man. The point we want to make is that your son was growing all along, but the changes were so small from day to day that you couldn't see them.

An example of a positive process would be learning to play a musical instrument such as the piano. Again, in keeping with the definition of process, the changes take place slowly over time. The small, daily improvements in skill may not be obvious, but after a few weeks of practice you will notice that you can play music which is significantly more difficult. This makes it hard to stay motivated to practice because the changes are so small from one day to the next.

How Processes Operate Within Families

There are many positive and negative processes that take place within families. Since this book is being written from a social learning perspective, our interest lies in describing the *changes that take place in the interactions between family members.* As it turns out, these changes take place as the result of the interactions family members have with one another. This means that family interactions are the mechanism driving the process, and these same interactions change slowly over time as a result of the process. Thus, our focus here is on exchanges between family members.

Returning to the question raised at the beginning of this chapter, parents find themselves with problem children on their hands because certain disruptive processes have been operating within their families for months, or even years. When these processes go unchecked, the outcomes can be very dramatic over time. But the day-to-day manifestations of the process are so subtle that it is difficult to see them. The changes taking place are small enough that the only way we can see them is to look at very detailed data describing the interactions between family members. Parents do not have this type of high-quality data to assist them in detecting destructive processes that are chipping away at the foundation of their happiness. Sometimes this means that children turn into little monsters before the parents realize what is going on, and then they are at a loss for understanding how their happy family could have turned out this way. This chapter outlines a very destructive process we call "coercion" that makes a primary contribution to the disruption of families. Coercion, and the related concept of escalation, are not easy to present in simple terms, but it is important for parents to understand how these mechanisms work. This awareness will help you to prevent these processes from tearing at the fabric of your family.

Processes that Disrupt Families

In most families the birth of a baby is a joyful occasion. As parents, we strive to provide our children with opportunities that we missed in our own childhoods. We want the best for them and hope that they will be happy. How is it then, with all of this loving and dreaming, that roughly one infant in 10 will become a delinquent adolescent with three or more police offenses? We believe that coercion and other disruptive processes make a primary contribution to delinquency and other conduct problems in adolescents. While elements of these processes operate within all families, some families become more immersed in them than others. In the case of delinquency, the children are taught (inadvertently) to be abrasive in the way they treat other family members. As part of their training they learn to be verbally abusive, and occasionally have outbursts that include hitting siblings and even parents. As unlikely as it may seem, they are also *trained* to avoid work and other responsibilities. It is counterintuitive to think that parents teach their children to be antisocial or irresponsible, or that spouses teach each other to hurt the other person in order to get what they want. We will see how this training takes place later in this chapter.

Most families start out with the mother and father feeling good about each other. The newlyweds are convinced that no one else has ever shared *their* kind of love before, that they are unique among the millions of marriages that have taken place. They are sincere when they say their love will last forever. However, the fact is that for most couples these feelings of love slowly erode into a kind of grey and lifeless acceptance of something less. For others, the change is more dramatic. Studies show that about one out of every four couples shifts from loving to hitting. How does this come about? We believe that a good part of it is the outcome of increasingly unpleasant exchanges between spouses. It is like a dance where the partners nudge each other toward becoming increasingly negative in how they treat one another. Simple disagreements shift to hostile comments, to bitter arguments, then to shouting and threatening matches, to throwing things, and finally to hitting. (This is what we call "escalation," which will be discussed later in this chapter). In fact, systematic studies of thousands of American families by two eminent sociologists, Steinmetz & Straus, led them to conclude that "marriage is a license to hit."(1) They also mentioned that in many families hating was more likely than loving! Neither of these ideas fits the stereotype of what the typical American family is like. Most of us would be very surprised if we were told that we would eventually hit our spouse. However, disruptive processes are easily introduced into any social setting.

Coercion

The term "coercion" means using unpleasant behaviors to get what you want. In families, this means nagging, yelling, throwing tantrums, and using other disagreeable behaviors to bring about a desired result such as getting the children to clean up their rooms. In most families there is evidence of coercion being used to change the behavior of other family members. Some families reserve these tactics for extreme situations, others routinely use yelling and screaming. Our research indicates that there are some dire consequences for using coercion on a regular basis. Unfortunately, family members often fall into the trap of using unpleasant behaviors with one another at high rates. We have found several reasons why this happens.

One reason coercion is used in families is that it is an effective way to get things done. Being hostile and screaming at the children to clean up their rooms usually results in at least a brief flurry of action. But there are a number of side effects: 1) The children may start avoiding their parents, or

231

lying to them. When this happens, parents do not know what their children are doing, so it is difficult to punish them when they do something inappropriate. This means that the parents lose some control, and that the children are learning to be good liars. 2) One hostile comment is usually followed by another. This approach is almost guaranteed to start an argument or a fight which can escalate into a major confrontation. 3) Using unpleasant responses like screaming and threatening creates distance between parents and children. It is hard for parents and children to "bond" with each other if they are constantly enmeshed in arguments and shouting matches. It takes time for family members to recover from an exchange like this. During this time, positive exchanges are unlikely since each party feels the victim of an injustice (the parent feels he or she "had to" yell at the children because they didn't respond to a reasonable request made earlier, and the children feel that they have been treated badly). 4) Perhaps worst of all, the parents are likely to yell at the children in the future when it comes time to get them to do something like homework or room cleaning because the yelling worked! The children also learn to be hostile or use sarcasm because they have learned that this is an acceptable way to act when they are upset or want someone to do something in a hurry. Thus, this simple exchange has changed the behavior of everyone involved; but the changes are destructive. Parent/child relationships and mother/father relationships are damaged by these exchanges. When coercion is routinely used in families, the changes can become very dramatic.

Punishment is related to coercion because it relies on the use of unpleasant events to change behavior. It also produces immediate changes in ongoing behavior and there are side-effects to using punishment too often. One major difference between them is that there are times when it is appropriate to use punishment, whereas coercion is *never* acceptable.

Punishment and coercion are compared in more detail later in this chapter, but the point we wish to make here is that parents pay a heavy price for controlling family members with unpleasant events.

At our research center we use the term "pain control" as a way of talking about the impact of extremely unpleasant responses on family interactions. The bad feelings created by a hostile comment or someone yelling at you may not seem to be in the same category as an electric shock or bamboo slivers under the fingernails, but the consequences are very similar. This chapter emphasizes the perils of pain control. Pain control is an extremely effective way to change behavior because it feels so good when the pain stops. Within families, the use of pain control is like using subtle torture—the pain is administered at increasingly intense levels (yelling turns to screaming, etc.) until the victim gives in Then the pain stops.

There are several reasons why pain control is such a frequent visitor in unhappy families. One of the primary reasons is that it is a very effective way to bring about a desired response over the short term. When we are exposed to painful stimuli, we are biologically wired to do whatever is necessary to turn the pain off. This takes place automatically, without awareness. Most of us don't think of sarcastic comments and hostile looks as being painful to others, but they are. And other family members tend to react in kind—a hostile comment is usually followed by a hostile response. The exchange of interpersonal hostilities often continues until one person turns up the intensity and the other person gives in. When this takes place in families, the daily skirmishes create an atmosphere filled with unresolved conflicts. Family members gradually change one another by brutal tactics that bring an end to happiness and good feelings toward one another.

Coercion Sequences

Coercion sequences teach family members to hurt one another. With sufficient practice, these exchanges become simple reflexive reactions.(2) There are two key principles involved in coercion sequences. First, an unpleasant response is used until it produces an immediate change in the behavior of the other person. Second, coercion almost always involves escalation when the family members are well rehearsed. Escalation means turning up the level of pain, often abruptly, to get the other person to give in. The thing to keep in mind is that during this exchange *each person teaches the other and the training is taking place with pain not love*.

Let's suppose this has been a long, hard day for a mother who comes home feeling tired and irritable. When she comes through the front door, the stereo is on full blast. The mother wants some peace and quiet, so she pleasantly asks her teenage daughter to turn down the stereo, but there is no response. She repeats her request to turn down the stereo two more times, but still there is no response. This time, with a rising pitch and an edge to her voice she storms into the family room and shouts, "I've already asked you three times to turn the stereo down. Now shut the damned thing off or I'll throw it through the window! That'll solve the problem once and for all!" (This is escalation on the mother's part.) The daughter responds by grumbling something the mother can't quite hear, and reluctantly turns off the stereo. Then the daughter slinks into her bedroom and stays there for the rest of the evening. In this instance, the mother's escalation from requesting, to nagging, to shouting and threatening worked.

The original problem was to get the adolescent to turn down her stereo. Asking her pleasantly to turn it down didn't work and neither did nagging, perhaps because the daughter has learned that her mother doesn't really expect

234

her to comply until she gets angry. When the yelling and threatening began, the girl gave in, which had the unfortunate effect of *reinforcing* the mother for escalating her attack. The adolescent was also reinforced (negatively) for complying to high intensity threats.

The Coercion Sequence

Example 1

THE SITUATION: The adolescent daughter was playing the stereo too loudly at a time when the mother wanted some peace and quiet. This is the sequence that followed:

Step 1 Mother	Step 2 Daughter	Step 3 Mother	Step 4 Daughter	END RESULT Mother
Requests (3 times)	No response	Yells & threatens	Turns off stereo	Stops yelling & threatening
—how each event is experienced by the other person—				
(–) to child	(–) to mother	(–) to child	(+) to mother	Pain stops for mother & child
				Mother "wins," and is more likely to yell and use threats in same situation

Coercion begins when someone introduces an unpleasant event into ongoing family exchanges. It is like throwing a

235

rock into a quiet little pond—the waves reverberate for quite a while. But the final sequence of events is what really counts in these exchanges. Look very carefully at the third step in the sequence. The mother escalated the intensity of her requests in order to get the daughter to pay attention. Because that worked (the daughter turned off the stereo), the mother was reinforced for yelling and threatening. This means that in the future, when the mother really wants something done, she will probably escalate the intensity of her request. The teenager, too, has learned that the best way to escape when Mom blows her lid off is to simply do the inevitable and shut the stereo off. The net result of this sequence is that the tendency for the mother to shout and use threats is *strengthened*. Coercion works because it changes things in the immediate situation. When a behavior is strengthened or reinforced it means that it is likely to occur again given the same set of circumstances. In this example *the adolescent taught the parent to get angry and shout, and the parent taught the adolescent to comply with a request after the parent becomes angry and shouts a threat.*

The short-term consequence of the mother yelling was that the stereo was turned off. This made the mother feel better. But in the long run, after hundreds of encounters like this, the daughter learns to procrastinate and drag her feet until the mother's voice reaches a certain shrill pitch and then the daughter rewards the mother for her irritability by giving in. This means that when the mother politely asks people to do something, she is ignored until she raises her voice and acts like a fishwife. On each occasion it works for her in the short run, but in the long run she becomes a nagging, angry person—the type of person she never wanted to be. The daughter also learns to be noncompliant when adults ask her to do something; it is best to wait to see if the intensity of the request escalates which indicates that they really mean it. In order to change this destructive process

236

where family members bring out the worst in each other, it is necessary to 1) reduce the rate of unpleasant events in the family, and 2) teach your adolescents to quickly comply with your reasonable requests. The steps outlined earlier in this book will help you do this.

In keeping with social learning principles, the changes in behavior that take place from a *process* like this are so gradual that no one notices them on a day-by-day basis. Months later the mother may notice that she is doing a lot of yelling and feels angry most of the time. She will probably say to herself, "Well, they make me do it, it's not my fault. They never do what I ask unless I yell and shout." And, in a way, she's right. Inadvertently, each member of the family has contributed to the unpleasant social environment.

Punishment Sequences

Punishment sequences are somewhat like coercion sequences in that the key element is unpleasant behavior. But there is one big difference. The effect of punishment sequences is to weaken or *stop* behaviors, while coercion sequences strengthen or *start* new behaviors (shouting and threatening in the earlier example). Thus, the long range impact of punishment and coercion sequences are just the opposite.

Let's assume this time that your adolescent is a chronic dawdler. He is such an expert at dragging his heels that he could take all day getting to a three-alarm fire and still make it seem like he gave it his best shot. He is especially talented at dawdling when it comes to doing his homework or his chores. The typical scene goes something like this: You have already asked him to do his homework, but nothing happened. Again, you ask him politely, "OK, Champ, it's time to put an hour in on the books now." This reasonable request is met with an adolescent explosion, "You guys are always after me—you treat me like a little kid. You don't even know if I *have* any homework. Nag, Nag, NAG! I can't stand living in this damn house!" Then he storms into his room and slams the door. You back off and let it go. The punishment sequence goes like this:

The Punishment Sequence

Example 2

THE SITUATION: You ask your adolescent son to do his homework.

Step 1 Child	Step 2 Parent	END RESULT Child
Has a temper tantrum	Stops asking	Tantrum stops

——How this is experienced by the other person——

(–) to parent	(+) to adolescent	Adolescent "wins," parent less likely to ask about homework

In this punishment sequence, an unpleasant response (the temper tantrum) is used by the adolescent to stop the parent from asking him to do his homework. The tantrum also makes it less likely that the parent will ask him to do his homework in the future. The parent reinforced the adolescent for the tantrum by removing the event that was unpleasant for him (requesting him to do his homework). Both of the people involved in this exchange have been changed by the process. The adolescent learned to have tantrums more often (by negative reinforcement), and the parent learned not to make requests about homework (the parent was punished for making the request). Punishment sequences such as this are usually very effective—they do not have to be repeated very often to change behavior.

The example above is not what most people would expect when they think about punishment. An example that fits the more commonplace notion about punishment would be the following. Let's suppose that a mother comes home from work and finds that her adolescent boy is not home. The agreement was that he was supposed to stay home and do his homework first, but he took it upon himself to go visiting his friends instead. The mother decides to remove telephone privileges for the day as a punishment for not staying home and doing homework.

Another Punishment Sequence

Example 3

THE SITUATION: The mother has told her adolescent son to do homework after coming home from school.

Step 1 Adolescent	Step 2 Mother	END RESULT Adolescent
Leaves house without doing homework	Removes telephone privileges for the day	Less likely to ignore parent's request to do homework

——How this is experienced by the other person——

(–) to mother	(–) to adolescent	mother "wins"

In this example, the mother is trying to teach her son to do his homework before going out to visit friends. When he failed to do this, she punished him by using an unpleasant event (removal of telephone privileges for the day). The next time the same situation occurs, the son will think twice about going out to visit friends before doing his homework.

Comparing Punishment and Coercion

To compare punishment and coercion sequences, let's

look at how a temper tantrum works in another exchange between family members. Let's say your daughter has promised her friends that she will be driving the family car tonight. Her father has just reminded her that she lost car privileges this week because she broke the rules for car use last week. The daughter's response is a high-pitched appeal to her mother. "But Mom, I promised my friends that I would pick them up at six. We have to go to the library for that special report. Would you *please* talk to Dad!" The mother refuses, and the daughter begins to yell about her rights as a member of the family and as a human being, and starts slamming doors and pushing chairs. The tantrum stops when Dad comes in and snarls, "Oh for God's sake, take the damned car and give us a little peace."

The coercion and punishment sequences went like this:

Example 4

THE SITUATION: The adolescent daughter asks to use the car; Dad reminds her that she has lost car privileges for the week.

Step 1 Daughter	Step 2 Mom	Step 3 Daughter	Step 4 Dad	END RESULT Daughter
Asks Mom for car	Says no	Has tantrum	Gives in	Gets to use the car—tantrum stops.

——How this is experienced by the other(s)——

(−) to mom	(−) to daughter	(−) to both parents	(+) to daughter	(+) to both parents
		*1	*2	*3

*1 Mom and Dad punished for saying no—daughter increases intensity of request (has tantrum).

*2 Dad rewarded for giving in (negative reinforcement) because tantrum stops. Long-term effect—Dad more likely to give in when Daughter has tantrum in future (learning via coercion).

*3 Daughter rewarded for having a tantrum—she "wins." Long-term effect—daughter is more likely to use tantrums again in the future when parents say no to something she wants.

As you can see, the chain of unpleasant events initiated by the daughter who wants to use the car resulted in an *immediate* change of behavior on the part of the parents. The daughter's tantrum was the key element in both the punishment sequence and the coercion sequence. It is important to note that in these sequences, *the daughter trained the parents*. In the punishment sequence (Steps 1-3) both parents were trained to *stop* telling the daughter she couldn't use the car. The exchange turned into a coercion sequence when the parents gave in to the daughter's tantrum and let her use the car (Step 4). This trained the parents to *start* giving in when the daughter has a tantrum because that is one way to stop the tantrum immediately (end result). This illustrates an essential difference between punishment and coercion sequences—punishment sequences teach people to *stop* doing something (saying no to the daughter's request to use the car), whereas coercion sequences teach people to *start* doing something (giving in to the daughter's requests). It is also clear from the examples above that punishment and coercion are related techniques (they are both embedded in the same exchange between family members). In fact, our research has shown that people who use a lot of one also use a lot of the other. Both sequences derive their power in terms of changing or initiating behavior from the contingent presentation of unpleasant behavior or events.

If the parents had stood their ground at Step 2, this exchange would have turned into a punishment sequence in which the daughter was taught that if she doesn't follow the rules for using the car, she loses car privileges for a week. Step 3 was the turning point. The parents should have imposed a consequence (such as a short work chore) for the daughter's tantrum. By giving in to the tantrum the whole learning situation was turned upside down—the mother and father were trained to stop being good parents!

A Contingent Relationship

In these four examples of punishment and coercion, there was a *contingent* relationship between what the children and adults did. This means that the unpleasant events, which are the key in these exchanges, occurred *in response to something the other person did*. As we discussed in an earlier chapter, a contingent relationship between behaviors or events means that *when* x occurs, *then* y follows. In the first example, the son used a tantrum to change the behavior of his parents (he stormed off into his room, and his parents stopped nagging about homework). *When* his parents asked about his homework, *then* the boy had a tantrum. This is similar to the last example in which the daughter used a tantrum to coerce her parents into letting her use the car. *When* the parents told her no, *then* the daughter had a tantrum. This is also a good example of a contingent relationship between parent and adolescent behavior. In both cases, the behavior of the parents involved in the exchange was changed by the contingent response of the adolescents.

The fact that the adolescents are actually more in control of the situation than the adults is surprising to most parents. The common assumption is that most of what is going on in families is more like Example 3, in which the adolescent son is punished by the mother for not doing his homework. Here, the mother's response is also contingent upon what the son has or has not done, but the mother is in control rather than the adolescent. Our research indicates that in severely disrupted families, most of the training is of the former rather than the latter variety. It is relatively easy to see that when adolescents train their parents through coercive means, the outcome is very destructive. The parents are punished for trying to discipline their adolescents and are rewarded for giving in (by negative reinforcement). The reactions of the parents to what their teenagers are doing teach the teenagers to use tantrums to get what they want. The net result of all this is that the adolescents become increasingly out of control and unpleasant to be around.

Long-Term Versus Short-Term Consequences

The short-term consequences of using unpleasant events such as temper tantrums, yelling, and threats is that people get what they want right away. In each of the four examples just described, the responses of the family members were intended to stop ongoing unpleasant behaviors as soon as possible. It is easy to see why family members would react this way. But there are several long-term consequences for allowing people (children, spouses, parents) to use unpleasant events to control the behavior of other family members. They can use punishment to make you *stop* doing something they don't like, and use coercion to get you to *start* doing something else. The short-term consequence is that you try to turn off the pain by giving in to them, but the long-term consequence is that you and the other person are being changed and your lives are becoming increasingly unpleasant. Because temper tantrums, yelling, and threatening work, people slip into the habit of using them *more often*. As this happens, everyone around them must learn to give in

243

or do whatever it takes to avoid the temper tantrums and the threats.

Awareness

The effects of using too much punishment or coercion aren't obvious from one day to the next. Over a period of time, however, the consequences can be very dramatic. At some point you begin to realize that you are yelling at your children all of the time, but they are still spoiled or out-of-control. They don't do their chores and they have mini-tantrums when they don't get what they want. The long-term consequences for using unpleasant events (or the threat of them) to control what other family members do are disastrous. In fact, most of the troubled families we see at our research center have drifted into this style of interacting with one another. In these families there are very few pleasant exchanges between the family members, and there are lots of unpleasant ones. When this happens, everyone in the family begins to notice that the feelings of love for one another are gone. That is why it is so important to identify and stop the use of pain control as soon as possible.

We believe that most people slip into the use of coercion and punishment sequences without giving it much thought. The first couple of times unpleasant behavior is used contingently to control others, it usually passes without much fanfare. Other family members are likely to label the behavior as being "feisty" or a little irritable. Most people make up stories to explain why things have to be this way. They tell themselves and others they wouldn't yell or fight all the time if other people didn't *make* them do it. In a peculiar sense they are right—other people did train them to be that way. But it is unnecessary to act this way, and the behavior must be stopped in order to avoid the long-term consequences that are very destructive to families.

Children and their parents have hundreds of social interactions every day. Most of the exchanges are very short, lasting perhaps three or four seconds. Very few of these interactions last for as long as a few minutes. In one study involving hundreds of families, the average encounter between mothers and their preadolescent children lasted only 18 seconds!

Social learning is concerned with encounters of the briefest kind. Most interactions where learning is taking place occur without anyone noticing them. During the dismal exchanges that lead to interpersonal aggression between family members (that is, using punishment and coercion sequences), most participants can identify only that they don't like each other very much. Each person would have a story to tell you explaining why it is necessary to be aggressive with the other person; for example, "The only way I can keep him from coming home late is to scream and yell at him." Neither side can see that over time each person plays an important part in teaching the other person to become more extreme.

Most of us are unaware of this *process* because the changes take place in tiny steps over a long period of time. The beautiful biological computer that each of us possesses is busy tracking and processing matters of greater importance. The social learning exchanges involved in this process are simply too trivial to be noticed. It is also true that the perceptual mechanisms of the brain are designed to attend primarily to dramatic changes in the environment. For example, if the temperature in the room where you are reading this book changed very gradually in the space of an hour or two you probably wouldn't be aware that anything was happening. You might notice a big difference after a while, but you wouldn't notice the tiny shifts until the cumulative effect was fairly dramatic. If the change happened suddenly while you were reading this book, you would notice it right away. It is easy to see why it is an efficient strategy for the brain to filter out stimuli that are relatively constant—this allows us to focus on dramatic changes requiring immediate responses. This may be part of the reason why it is so difficult for parents to notice the little changes that take place in family interactions as a result of punishment and coercion sequences.

Another contributing factor is that parents generally don't pay much attention to their children's behavior. Studies have shown that when parents are asked how many times relatively simple behaviors occur (such as whining and tantrums), their estimates are off by as much as 600%!(3) Studies of spouse conflict have also shown that couples don't realize how often they fight, say negative things, use put downs, and so on. In general, people are not good observers of their own behavior or the behavior of others. This implies that although we are learning as the result of the hundreds of mundane interactions we have with family members (in the sense that our behavior changes), we have very little accurate information about the course of this learning. It has been noted by modern cognitive psychologists, however, that we do make up stories to fill in the gaps. All of us have a great deal to *say* to our friends and psychiatrists about who we are and how we got that way.(4) But we don't notice the small changes that take place on a day-by-day basis in the way family members relate to one another.

How Does the Process Start?

When coercion and punishment sequences creep into adult relationships it is often due to outside stresses. Financial problems, working too much, illness, worrying, and dealing with necessities of raising a family all tend to take their toll. The connection between outside stressors and increases in parental irritability has been fairly well established.(5) The paradox is that when people are stressed out and need support, they tend to drive others away with their irritable behavior. Stressed out people give more commands, use more punishment and are more coercive in their interactions with others.(6) This means it is very easy for parents who are under a great deal of stress to set the whole coercion process into motion.

If someone under stress becomes irritable with you, it is the most natural thing in the world to assume that the irritable behavior is occurring *because of something you have done*. The next step in the process is to *respond* to this unpleasant behavior with irritable behavior of your own, which provides a tremendous boost to the coercion process. We have found in our own family that the best way to respond to someone who is stressed out is to ask, "Are you mad at me? What have I done to make you so upset?" The other person is often surprised to have their behavior labeled in this way, and the response is usually something like this, "No, I'm sorry (apologies are definitely appropriate here). You are the last person in the world I want to attack. I've just had a bad day at work, and I didn't get much sleep last night because I kept ruminating about it." This sort of response makes it possible for the other person to offer some support, since he or she is not being attacked, which defuses the situation.

All it takes to start the coercion process with children is for the parents to stop paying careful attention to what is going on with their own irritable behavior and that of other family members, and to relax their use of effective discipline for a few weeks. We believe that infants do not need to have someone teach them how to be irritable. When something bothers them, they frown and fuss, cry and sometimes scream. That is nature's way of insuring their survival and making sure that parents attend to their needs. But as they grow older, social survival depends upon their ability to learn substitutes for these primitive behaviors. (This was discussed in detail in Chapter 1: "Teaching Compliance and the Readiness to be Socialized.") Even if some of us have constitutional differences that partially determine our threshold for making irritable responses, everyone can learn to refrain from using pain control.

We believe that some problem children may have been difficult as infants (there are differences in temperament among infants). If the parents were unskilled and/or trying to deal with multiple stressors such as financial problems, unemployment, health problems, separation, and divorce, then there is a good chance they will use coercion and punishment sequences with their children. They may also fail to teach their children more appropriate techniques to get what they want and need.

Key Ideas in this Chapter (Unit One)

1. Processes are characterized by changes that take place slowly. This makes processes difficult to observe on a daily basis, but over time the outcomes can be dramatic.
2. Coercion is a destructive process that operates in most families. It involves exchanges between family members in which one person uses an unpleasant behavior or event to train the other person to give in. Coercion sequences teach people to *start* doing something (in this case, to start giving in when the other person uses unpleasant events).
3. Punishment sequences involve exchanges in which unpleasant events or behaviors are used to teach people to *stop* doing something.
4. Punishment and coercion sequences are similar in that unpleasant events are the key element. Punishment sequences are a necessary part of family life if they are not used too often or inappropriately. Coercion sequences are never acceptable because they strengthen unpleasant behaviors like yelling and temper tantrums. The use of

coercion, or misuse of punishment, can erode family happiness and contribute to adjustment problems in children.

5. There is a tremendous difference between the short-term and long-term consequences of using punishment and coercion sequences in families. Over the short term, you get what you want. But over the long term, family members teach one another to use unpleasant behaviors and events to control others. In most cases family members are not aware that their lives are becoming increasingly unpleasant.

Family Processes— Slow Changes, Dramatic Outcomes
Unit 2

Escalation

So far, we have introduced two main ideas. One is that coercion sequences use pain to strengthen behavior, while punishment sequences use pain to stop behavior. The other idea is that there are simultaneous (but strikingly different) short-term and long-term consequences for these sequences, and people generally don't notice the changes that are taking place because they happen so gradually.

If nothing is done to interrupt the process, then family members become locked into daily rounds of mini-fights. They take turns at starting fights, and they take turns at winning or losing them. As this happens, family members gradually slip into the habit of using unpleasant events at high rates.

Escalation is a concept that is intimately tied into the coercion process. This term refers to the increase in intensity that usually takes place as the disruptive episodes between family members get longer and longer over time. During heated exchanges, neither person is willing to give in easily, and both sides end up inflicting more and more pain on the other. In many cases, the exchange ends when one of the people involved in it turns up the intensity and says or does something that *really* hurts the other person, who then withdraws.

How does a process that is so destructive to families begin? Is it something that could happen to *any* normal family, or do the parents in disrupted families set out to be this way? In order to consider escalation from a developmental perspective, let's consider the example of a happy, young married couple. A year after the ceremony, they give birth to their first child and the wife quits her job. This abruptly reduces the number of positive social contacts for the mother, and the satisfaction she derived from her job skills and salary. Although there are many joys associated with being a new parent, some of them are bittersweet. Infants are very demanding, and caring for their needs is a full-time job with few rewards. A baby can never be left alone, which makes it difficult for the mother to see her friends, and now she doesn't have the time to do the things that she once enjoyed. The only time she gets out on her own is to run errands and do the grocery shopping. This means there is a dramatic decrease in positive experiences. At the same time, the mother's support network is substantially reduced because she has less contact with her friends. Over a period of months she becomes increasingly dissatisfied and begins to be irritable with her husband.

He, on the other hand, is totally immersed in the problem of making a living to support his family. He is very competent at his job, and has a good relationship with the people he works with. When he comes home he is greeted by an angry wife and an infant who is fussy and difficult to manage. To him, home is a place where problems accumulate during the day. Gradually, he begins to feel uninvolved in the family, and he finds himself avoiding his wife and resenting the baby. He misses the romance and closeness he had with his wife before the baby was born.

This isolates the mother even more, and removes one of her only sources of positive contact. When she is unpleasant, he is unpleasant in return, and the irritable exchanges between them become more pronounced. Occasionally, one of them will become concerned enough about the way things are going to try to improve the situation, but this is usually short-lived. All it takes is a little stress and the destructive process begins right where it left off.

Now both people are caught up in the process. When she nags, he attacks her for being incompetent and ungrateful; after all he is out there in the real world working while she just stays at home and takes care of the baby. The coercion sequences grow longer and become more intense (this is escalation). With practice, each person gets better at hurting the other. It becomes increasingly difficult to communicate how hurt and angry each of them feels, and the other person also becomes less receptive to hearing about it. The hurting and the arguing escalate further. Now there is very little effort being made to solve the problems that started the process and feed into it. The focus has shifted from loving to hurting the other person. The couple does fewer fun things together. The ratio of positive to negative experiences gets more and more out of balance. Who wants to play with someone who has become an enemy!

Now the husband and the wife have both discovered that the best way to "win" an argument or shouting match is to suddenly increase the intensity by doing or saying something outrageous that really hurts the other person. This has a powerful effect in that the other person almost always withdraws and the fight ends (at least for the time being). But, in the long run, both people lose. Each person becomes an expert in capitalizing on the areas where the other person is vulnerable. Using powerful weapons insures an immediate victory. The sweet taste of victory is short lived, because in the next round the *other* person reciprocates by escalating until a win is scored. The battles go back and forth—and each person becomes increasingly adept at inflicting pain on the other.

The mechanism here is the same as the one involved in coercion sequences. This time it is:

The Escalation Sequence

Step 1	Step 2	END RESULT
person A is irritable	person B uses a high-intensity un-pleasant response	person A gives in, the pain stops

Person A learns to give in; Person B learns to escalate the intensity of unpleasant responses.

The increase in intensity can involve words intended to hurt the other person, but eventually, it may escalate to include throwing things and hitting. Thus, abusive behavior is sometimes the outcome of low-intensity coercive family processes that start with things like angry looks, sarcastic comments, and a hostile tone of voice. Over time these responses become part of an escalating process that changes the dynamics between family members so drastically that people lose control of themselves. At this point, hurting one another becomes a simple, reflexive act. As the behavior of each person changes, both the husband and the wife make up stories to explain to themselves and their friends why they are doing these things. The stories generally reflect an overall tendency to view the other person in an increasingly negative light.

Alcohol is one of the variables that seems to speed up the escalation process. Many of the reported instances of spouse abuse (and physical assault in general) occur when one or both parties have been drinking.

Escalation also is involved in the parent/adolescent struggles that are generated by punishment and coercion sequences. Remember the first example where the mother made her daughter turn off the stereo by threatening to throw it through the window? In this situation, the sudden escalation on the mother's part was effective. The daughter lost that round, but you can bet that the war will not end here. Many battles are yet to be waged by both sides before the trumpets of conquest are silenced.

Parents should be the ones in control; and it is up to them to take the steps necessary to prevent coercion sequences and inappropriate punishment sequences from occurring in their families (or to change things if they notice the process starting). Here are several suggestions that will help you do this in your own family. Be sure to make requests in a neutral or pleasant manner. If the child does not comply with your request, immediately provide a negative consequence. In the example of the mother and the stereo, she started off on the right foot when she asked the daughter to turn down the stereo. When this request was ignored, as were the two that followed, she could have solved the problem by walking into the family room and (calmly) turning it off, then announcing in a firm but neutral tone of voice that the stereo would now have to stay off for 30 minutes. This would have made the confrontation with her daughter unnecessary (unless the daughter decided to push the point).

Intervening immediately in the tiny skirmishes that happen every day in families prevents family members from starting up the escalation ladder where unpleasant interchanges become increasingly tense. It is very important to change things early in the process so that the emotional levels stay within a reasonable range. If you try to put an end to the dance of pain when both sides are very upset, it is much more likely that one side or the other will lose control.

Unpleasant Events in Family Life

As we went into homes to study how family members interact with one another, we noticed there was an enormous range of things we might call unpleasant events. In some families, "doing" something unpleasant to a family member almost always involved words. In other families, nonverbal behaviors such as scowls, gestures, glares and so forth have special meanings that are powerful. Table 7.1 is a list of the code categories we use in our research to keep track of events that most people would agree are unpleasant. The events selected for this table occur often enough to make it worthwhile to count them; these are the minor hurtful things that family members do to each other on a daily basis. While the list does not cover everything that goes into coercive exchanges, it is a representative sample.

Table 7.1
AVERSIVE EVENTS USED BY FAMILY MEMBERS

Code Categories	Definitions
Command Negative	A command in which immediate compliance is demanded, aversive consequences threatened, and sarcasm or humiliation is directed toward the receiver.
Cry	Whining or sobbing sounds.
Disapproval	Verbal or gestural criticism of another person's behavior or characteristics.

256

Dependency	When a person is obviously capable of doing a task by him- or herself, but requests assistance.
Destructive	When a person damages, soils, or breaks something.
High Rate	Physically active, repetitive behavior which is likely to be annoying.
Humiliate	Embarrassing, shaming, or making fun of another person.
Ignore	Intentional and deliberate nonresponse to an initiated behavior.
Noncomply	When a person does not do what is requested in response to a command, command negative, or a dependency within 12 seconds of the request being made.
Negativism	A neutral verbal message delivered in a tone of voice which conveys an *attitude* of "Don't bug me." Also included are defeatist statements.
Physical Negative	Physical attack or attempt to attack another person (hitting, shoving, etc.).
Tease	The act of annoying, pestering, mocking, or making fun of another person.
Whine	Using a slurring, nasal, or high-pitched voice. The content of the statement is irrelevant.
Yell	Shouting, yelling, or talking loudly.

We can all see little bits and pieces of ourselves as we examine this list—many of them are things that probably occur in your home. Some of the items on the list, such as Whine and High Rate, are behaviors observed more often in children than adults (although some adults have a tendency to whine a fair amount, and others get high rate by running off at the mouth). For adults, the unpleasant behaviors that are the most likely to occur are telling people what to do and criticizing them. A normal mother is likely to do one or the other of these at least once every minute!

Each of us has our own style of using these behaviors, but most of us use them in a unplanned fashion. We simply *react* to something that someone has said, done, or not done. There is no underlying plan or intention, however, to change anyone's behavior. What we are doing instead in these situations is reflexively expressing our own irritation, like swatting at a house fly. People use disapproval, sarcasm, or arguing to let the world know they are displeased. There is quite a bit of variation in how much a given person uses these behaviors (and which ones are used) from one day to the next. Some of the variables that determine this are your mood, who you are interacting with, and how tired or upset you are. But usually these mini-conflicts do not go anywhere if the other person does not respond in kind. However, if the other person is under stress, or has had a bad day, then it is more likely that his or her response will be an angry one.

A Progression of Coercive Behaviors in Children

Our research shows that children move through a fairly predictable sequence or *progression* of coercive behaviors. That is, they start with behaviors which are mildly unpleasant, and move on to more extreme behaviors with time.

The first noticeable step in the progression is when children don't do as they are asked. When reasonable requests require major confrontations, the first step has been taken on an unfortunate journey. First, the child may find that ignoring requests is effective in avoiding responsibility. Next, the child begins to have temper tantrums. Gradually, the child learns that a good tantrum works even better than ignoring in getting the parent to stop making requests. The temper tantrums occur more often and become increasingly intense. When such children (especially boys) enter school, they are ready to take the next step, which is fighting with other children. At first, it is easy to rationalize why this might be so ("He's the new kid at school," or "Boys will be boys."). Time goes by and now you notice that unexplained items are turning up at the house and in the yard. When the child is confronted about these things, he explains that, "Jimmy gave me his truck," or "Johnny let me borrow his Transformers for the weekend." More time passes and now there are reports that lunch money is missing from children's desks at school, and perhaps the local convenience store calls to inform you that your son has been picked up for shoplifting. You find it hard to believe that this could be so, since you have always given him what he wanted, and he could do his chores for some extra spending money if he needed it. After several experiences with problems such as disobedience, fighting, and stealing you realize that you are not managing your child's behavior very well. The warning signs were there all along, but you chose to ignore them when they first appeared. Parents don't want to believe they have a problem child on their hands, but the description presented above emphasizes the importance of looking as objectively as possible at your child's behavior. If people are telling you that your child has conduct problems, you should listen to what they have to say.

THE COERCION PROGRESSION

   Noncompliance

                  Temper tantrums

                                Fighting

                                          Stealing

As indicated by this progression, some really noncompliant children also tend to have frequent temper tantrums (about once a week for 10-year-olds). A smaller number of children who have frequent temper tantrums also tend to hit people. The hitting occurs at home with siblings and at school with other children. What is interesting about this is that most 10-year-old children who have temper tantrums *do not* go on to become frequent hitters. But almost all "fighters" have tantrums.

Only a small number of children steal, but the majority who do steal have been fighters and have frequent tantrums. Many of the fighter-stealers go on to have a record of several police offenses by the time they are in their teens. This emphasizes the importance of stopping the coercion progression before it becomes a serious problem for the child, the parents, and everyone else involved. We believe that this progression of problem behaviors is a direct outcome of the training the child received in the home, and that this training takes place in homes where coercion and punishment sequences occur regularly.

There is nothing inevitable about the coercion process. The key idea from social learning theory is that *children learn what to do and what not to do by their parents' contingent reactions to their behavior. It is not what you SAY, but what you DO that changes the behavior of other family members.* The household rule might be to say what you want once or twice so the children know what is acceptable and what is not. Following the rules should be encouraged

260

with positive attention, extra privileges, and other pleasant events. Breaking the rules should be dealt with by using contingencies such as loss of privileges to make the rules stick. Simply saying what you want without backing it up (that is, using contingent consequences) is usually not enough to change behavior.

Positive Reactions: The Other Side of the Coin

Your positive reactions to the good things your adolescent does also have a profound impact. These positive reactions are the other side of the same coin, and in a very real sense are more important to the dynamics that operate within healthy families than the coercive processes we have just discussed. The use of pain control poisons an atmosphere of love, and makes it difficult to interact with your family in a positive style. Managing the use of hurtful behaviors and preventing the escalation of these behaviors are viewed as prerequisites for establishing and maintaining positive interactions within families. It is the warm exchanges between family members that form the base for socializing children and helping them to learn important new skills, including those skills necessary for developing a good self-image and loving others.

We believe that what people actually do is governed by the outcomes their behaviors produce. When something is rewarded or reinforced, we tend to repeat it. If certain behaviors are ignored or punished then we are less likely to repeat them in the future. These two simple ideas are at the core of the social learning approach to understanding family dynamics.

Most of us believe that we know a great deal about rewards and reinforcement. But in the context of family interactions these words have a less obvious meaning, because we are dealing with barely noticeable events. Instead of a prize for the top golf score, it is a smile from across the dinner table. Instead of a trophy for an outstanding performance, a social reinforcer should be given for completing each of the many steps it takes to learn something difficult. Touching the shoulder of someone who tries for the one hundredth time to play the C scale on the family piano is part of what keeps that person going. When someone is learning a new skill, you can't expect a perfect performance. Mere approximations of the fully developed skill are worth rewarding. Each step toward the goal is noteworthy.

Attention, positive comments and nonverbal behaviors like smiles and hugs are small things, but they increase the likelihood that the behaviors which produced them will occur again in the future. One of the great parental myths of our time is that children do what they are supposed to because they know what parents want, and they strive to conform to those wishes out of an overbearing sense of filial duty. Most normal children are very clear about what their parents want them to do, yet they often do otherwise. Testing the rules and a little noncompliance are perfectly normal.

Using a positive approach to change behavior requires much effort and skill. But that is not the reason most parents do not use this approach. The reason is that it takes a long time to see the results of using rewards and reinforcers to change behavior—positive interactions produce such small effects that you don't see them unless you track them carefully (it is also a process). It would take you literally weeks or months of really *good* positive reinforcement to teach the "random thrower" to hang up his coat. That's pretty slow compared to using punishment, which works in as few as one or two trials. It is our hunch that parents fall into the habit of using punishment to change behavior because it is effective immediately.

Why not use punishment or coercion to change behavior? It is much faster in producing results. If you use an effective punishment each time your son forgets to hang up his coat, it would take only a few days for him to learn not to leave it lying around the house. Punishment teaches people to stop doing things right away. We have just discussed how coercion can be used to teach someone a new behavior. Again, the problem is that these techniques do get results over the short term, but over the long term, pain control carries a heavy price tag. It accelerates antisocial and out-of-control behavior, and makes it very difficult to have good relationships with your children. If you use pain control as the primary means of teaching your children what is appropriate and what is not, they will avoid you like the plague. An eminent sociologist named F. R. Bales observed hundreds of small groups and commented that, by far, groups made up of family members were more negative with each other than members of any of the other groups he had studied.(7) What a sorry state of affairs that is. Using reinforcement, on the other hand, has none of these negative side-effects. The changes it produces are slow, but using lots of praise and attention is a good way to build a strong relationship with your children. Instead of avoiding you, your children will seek you out and ask for your advice if you use a positive approach to raising them.

The Family Bank Account

The family is like a bank—people make deposits and withdrawals from their interpersonal accounts every day. Happy families, or good relationships among friends, are maintained by frequent deposits and occasional withdrawals. There must be some of both, with just the right balance.

Deposits are made when people provide love, support, and understanding for each other. Carrying out routine responsibilities like doing housework, going to work, and doing chores are also activities that contribute to the family's bank account. But all too often these important events receive very little recognition from family members. This is especially true in families who have slipped into the habit of taking one another's contributions for granted.

Withdrawals are made in a variety of ways, but in most cases they consist of the negative events that occur in families. Most people make their withdrawals unintentionally on a day-to-day basis. Nagging, being uncooperative, martyred sighs, vicious or humiliating remarks—any one of these puts a strain on things and therefore represents a withdrawal. When one or more family members withdraw more than they contribute, the family bank account becomes overdrawn and the love and good feelings between family members disappear.

It is reasonable, however, to make some withdrawals from the family bank account. Why make deposits if you can't get something back every now and then? Everyone needs some support and encouragement when things fall apart at work or at school, and it's nice to have people who really care about you to put you back on your feet. But the withdrawals shouldn't be wasted on irritable or hostile responses directed toward family members. These negative responses are usually unnecessary, and they drain the account quickly. It is better to save your withdrawals for a rainy day, when you really need an empathetic ear and a shoulder to cry on. Stressed out, hurting people need someone to understand their pain and to comfort them. These events are also withdrawals, but deposits can always be made later to bring the account back up to a healthy balance.

The bank account notion can be extended to include balances between people, as well as an accounting of positive versus negative events. People need to be able to give and to take from each other. In families, parents are *supposed* to

264

give more than they receive, particularly during the early years. (Many parents take this to extremes, however, and sacrifice themselves in the process. Even during the early years it is important to maintain a healthy balance—parents need to be happy in order to be good parents.) As children grow older, they should be expected to start making some substantial deposits to their interpersonal accounts. By the time adolescents are ready to leave home their interpersonal accounts should show a balance between deposits and withdrawals. This is an important skill that will help them get along with others in the outside world. It is the basis for forming good relationships with significant others.

Surprisingly enough, some people don't like to be on the receiving end because it obligates them to give something in return. They don't let their friends or family members help them during hard times because they don't want to seem weak or needy. These people are rejecting the idea of a bank account—they don't want to make withdrawals, which means they aren't obligated to make deposits either. For these solitary souls, hard times can only be endured through personal strength or will power. There is no reliance or dependence on outside people. Friends who might want to help are rebuffed. This means that friends and family are not allowed to ask for help either; since they are never permitted to make deposits, they don't have the right to make withdrawals. This is an unfortunate approach to life. There is much to be gained by sharing the good and the bad with others who are close to you; it makes the good times better, and the bad times easier to bear. Much of the satisfying texture in life is experienced in this way.

Giving too much to the family bank account can also create problems. People who do this often become bitter and disappointed in the long run. Many American women fall into this mode and become the resident family martyr. They make meals, run errands, and do things for others without expecting much in return. But eventually they find themselves feeling hurt because family members give them so little in return; they resort to using guilt at every opportunity. Now, when someone tries to make a deposit, the mother makes sarcastic comments or disparaging remarks such as, "It's about time that someone else vacuumed the living room!" Attempts to change the situation are met with rejection or a description of past failures.

When bank accounts become overdrawn, it is time to have some good experiences together. Take a vacation, or go away together for a weekend. Agree to put the problems you are having with family members on hold for a while until your reserves are built up again. Solving conflicts can usually be handled at another time. In our own family, both of us work full time. This means that pressure and stress can build up very quickly. We find it necessary to get away together every other weekend just to keep the deposits in our bank account at a level healthy enough to deal with stressful situations during the week. Overwork and stress accompanied by too little laughter and play tarnish even the best of relationships. The antidote for this is to do something fun together.

If your spouse or adolescent is irritable for several days running, it is a good idea to find out what is going on *before* the account is overdrawn. Try saying something like, "You seem upset. Is it something that I've done, or are there problems in your world?" This approach is simple and direct, and it labels for the other person what you see happening without accusations or assigning fault.

Irritable people who repeatedly overdraw their accounts may find themselves feared and avoided by family members, and it is unlikely that they will feel loved. These are often lonely and isolated people who attend family gatherings but are more or less a mystery to everyone else. Some of them report in therapy sessions that they would like to change, but they just can't help themselves. As they see it, there are so many people in the family that need correcting they have to act this way. ("After all, it's for their own good.") They continue to use pain control and, as a result, they go on being avoided and isolated members of the family.

Irritability and Adjustment Problems

It is our growing opinion that coercion and irritability are intimately involved in a wide range of pathologies found in families. There are also some findings from several large scale studies that support this idea. The Isle of Wight studies compared several hundred normal adolescents with adolescents who showed evidence of psychiatric problems.(8) The results of this study indicated that problem children were more likely to come from families with high rates of irritable exchanges between parents, *and* between parents and adolescents.

A survey study of this kind does not determine whether or not the irritable exchanges *caused* the adolescents' psychiatric problems. It is quite possible that simply having such a child in the home *causes* everyone (including the parents) to be more irritable in their interactions with each other. But parents are the ones responsible for raising children and making changes when things get out of control.

In one important study, researchers counted the irritable exchanges between adult psychiatric patients and members of their families.(9) These interviews were conducted prior to admitting the patient to the hospital for treatment. Later, when the patient had been treated and returned to the family, the researchers checked to see how the patients were adjusting. Patients who were returned to families with low rates of unpleasant and irritable behaviors did very well—only 16% returned to the hospital. But in families that used a lot of pain control, 58% of the patients returned to the hospital. This study has been replicated a number of times. The evidence from these studies suggests that living in coercive families decreases the chance that severely disturbed adult patients will successfully make the adjustment to living at home.

But the question remains, do coercive exchanges cause adolescent psychiatric problems? A longitudinal study being carried out at UCLA has followed up adolescents and their families who came to a mental health clinic for treatment. Their initial findings show a strong link between the rate of irritable exchanges observed among the family members when they were at the clinic and the development of extreme psychiatric adjustment problems later on.

We do not know that *all* families with high levels of irritable exchanges produce adolescents with adjustment problems. It seems unlikely that there is a one-to-one correspondence here. But the linkage is strong enough to lead us to believe that it should be brought to the attention of parents. It is neither necessary nor a good idea for family members to use irritable responses. If you want to check to see whether or not this is a problem in your family, turn on a tape recorder during the dinner hour; then play it back to see if you can find examples of family members being irritable with one another. To change this behavior, you will need to track it and set up some consequences for family members who are irritable in their interactions with others.

The Stranger Rule: Another Personal Bias

For many of us, the sharp, sarcastic comment delivered with a twist of humor is just part of the normal give and take within families. If you live in certain areas of the country, the conventional wisdom suggests that clever witticisms are a good way to toughen up children. After all, it's a push and shove world out there, and strangers are seldom gentle when they want something from you. We propose an alternative view. The daily use of unpleasant events to control the behavior of other family members can have a very unfortunate impact upon everyone in your family. Being negative and sarcastic is one of the features of your behavior that you should not allow to become automatic. Some people lash out at others in the same reflexive way they drive their cars—they do both without thinking very much about it.

There is perhaps a good reason for the emphasis on politeness that is found in many European populations. In Europe there are many people living in a small space. While most of us in America observe some rules of politeness or decorum while visiting the homes of others, in our own dwellings we change into full-blown coercive monsters. For each of the authors, bitter experience has taught us the importance of *not* using coercion. We have finally developed what Marion calls the "Stranger Rule": you should treat members of your family with the same respect and consideration that you would give to a stranger who was a guest in your home.

Again, this does not mean that we must always accept and endure the behavior of family members. There are noncoercive means for changing the behavior of family members that are effective, and yet do not disrupt normal family processes.

Key Ideas in this Chapter (Unit Two)

1. Escalation is a term describing the increase in intensity that characterizes unpleasant exchanges between family members.
2. There is a fairly predictable progression of coercive behaviors beginning with noncompliance and ending with more serious delinquent behaviors. The progression is not inevitable.
3. Positive responses are a very important part of the dynamics that operate in normal families. When parents respond positively to the children's behavior it encour-

ages bonding and builds self-esteem.

4. The bank account notion is a way to describe the cumulative effect of having fun together as a family, and the impact of using punishment or being irritable on the well-being of the family.

5. Irritability is associated with adjustment problems in children.

Chapter Seven References

1. Steinmetz, S. K. and Straus, M. A. (Eds.) *Violence in the Family*. New York: Dodd, Mead & Co., 1974.

2. Gottman, J. M. *A Couple's Guide to Communication*. Champaign, IL: Research Press, 1979.

3. Peine, H. *Behavioral Recording by Parents and its Resultant Consequences*. Unpublished Master's Thesis, University of Utah, 1970.

See Also

Herbert, E. *Parent Programs—Bringing it All Back Home*. Paper presented at the annual meeting of the American Psychological Association, Miami, 1970.

4. Tomkins, S. S. "Differential Magnification of Affects." In H. E. Howe, Jr., & R. A. Dienstbier (Eds.) *Nebraska Symposium on Modification*, Vol. 26. Lincoln, Nebraska: University of Nebraska Press, 1979.

5. See Chapter 10 in Patterson, G. R. *A Social learning Approach*, Volume 3: *Coercive Family Process*. Eugene, Oregon: Castalia Publishing Company, 1982.

See Also

Forgatch, M. S., Patterson, G. R., and Skinner, M. L. "A Mediational Model for the Effect of Divorce on Antisocial Behavior in Boys." In E. M. Heatherington & J. D.

Aresteh (Eds.) *Impact of Divorce, Single Parenting, and Stepparenting on Children*. In press.

6. Bell, D. (Ed.) *Lives in Stress: Women and Depression*. Beverly Hills, CA: Sage Publications, 1982.

7. Bales, R.F. "The Equilibrium Problem in Small Groups." In T. Parsons, R. Bales, & E. Shilo (Eds.), *Working Papers in the Theory of Action*. New York: Free Press, 1953.

8. Rutter, M., Tizard, J., and Whitmore, R. *Education, Health, and Behavior*. New York: John Wiley & Sons, 1970.

9. Brown, G. W., Birley, J. L., & Wing, J. K. "Influence of Family Life on the Course of Schizophrenic Disorders: A Replication." *British Journal of Psychology*, 1972, *121*, 241-258.

Glossary

Active listening means paying attention to what your children say. When your adolescent daughter says she had a bad day at school, you should stop what you are doing and get into her world for a while. Be sympathetic, and ask for more details in an unobtrusive way. Active listening refers to being involved in what your children are saying, rather than being passive and uninterested. Offering advice is not part of active listening.

The **"Antisocial Triad"** is made up of three behaviors: non-compliance, temper tantrums, and avoiding responsibility.

The term **back up** has both general and specific meanings. Generally, it refers to the follow-up consequences that parents impose to provide support for the positive or negative sanctions they use with adolescents. In this text, the term **back-up reward** means providing a weekly bonus if the teenager reaches the daily criterion a certain number of days per week on the point chart (this is discussed in detail in Chapter 5). The term **back-up punishment** means adding a negative consequence, such as privilege removal, if the teenager refuses to do a five-minute work chore that has already been assigned as punishment (this is described in detail in Chapter 6).

Coercion means using unpleasant behaviors to get what you want. Family members who use disagreeable behaviors such as nagging or yelling to teach other family members to start doing something (or to strengthen a behavior) are involved in the coercion process. Coercion derives its ability to change behavior through the contingent presentation of unpleasant events. The following is an example of how coercion is used in families: an adolescent son is asked to mow the lawn; the boy's response is to throw a tantrum; his parents respond by giving in instead of requiring him to do the work. In this example, the boy has taught his parents to give in when he throws a tantrum. The net result is that the boy "wins."

Compliance refers to whether or not children carry out the requests and commands their parents make. Compliance also implies a willingness to follow rules, and acting in a cooperative spirit.

A **contingent** arrangement implies a when/then connection between the adolescent's behavior and the parent's response. When the adolescent comes home late, then a work chore is imposed; when the adolescent takes care of certain responsibilities, then privileges are earned.

Irritability is testy, angry, or hostile behavior.

Monitoring refers to how well parents keep track of their adolescents' behavior away from home. In order to be effective as parents, it is necessary to know the answers to the FOUR BASIC QUESTIONS: who are your children with, where are they, what are they doing, and when will they be home?

Negative reinforcement is not defined in the text of this book because it is a difficult concept to explain in simple terms. Negative reinforcers also strengthen behavior but, unlike positive reinforcers (which we have simply referred to as "reinforcers" in this book), their ability to change behavior is based on the presentation of negative events that people want to avoid or terminate.

Negative reinforcement is effective in terms of maintaining or changing behaviors. An example of negative reinforcement we are all familiar with is the buzzer that sounds if your seatbelt is not fastened when you get in a car. *When* you fasten the seatbelt, *then* the irritating sound of the buzzer stops. This reinforces you for using the seatbelt. Infants who cry when their diapers are wet are using negative reinforcement to train their caretakers to attend to their needs; when their needs are met, then they stop crying. Negative reinforcement is a contingent arrangement.

The phrase **"pain control"** refers to the use of extremely unpleasant responses by family members to control the behavior of others.

Punishment is somewhat like coercion in that the key element is the contingent presentation of unpleasant events. The difference is that in punishment sequences these events decrease or weaken behaviors. The following is an example of how punishment is used in families: a father tells his adolescent daughter that she must finish her homework before she does anything else; the daughter does homework for five minutes and then calls her best friend on the telephone; the father hears her using the telephone and interrupts the call; he tells his daughter that she has just lost her telephone privileges for the day. In this example, the father used punishment to teach his daughter to stop engaging in distracting activities when she is supposed to be doing her homework.

A (positive) **reinforcer** is defined in terms of its effect on behavior. When a reinforcer follows a behavior, the behavior is strengthened. This is a contingent arrangement. A reinforcer is an event or thing that feels good to the person receiving it.

Social reinforcers are found in the behavior of other people. A smile, a nod of approval, or words of encouragement are examples of social reinforcers. **Nonsocial reinforcers,** on the other hand, are not derived from the behavior of other people. They are desirable things or events such as rewards, money, and privileges that can be used to strengthen behavior (they are also called "tangible rewards" because they tend to be visible events or things).

Socialization is the process of teaching children about the rules of society and how to respond appropriately to the people around them. Interacting directly with parents and other people is the primary vehicle for socialization, but children also learn vicariously by watching people interact with one another. Well-socialized children tend to follow the rules in a given setting, are liked by their peers, and are socially responsive. **The readiness to be socialized** refers to how receptive children are to learning new behaviors and skills from others.

Tracking means paying attention to specific adolescent behaviors. It involves breaking global concepts such as "bad attitude" into components that everyone can see.

Appendices

Appendix 1
A Very Brief History of the Social Learning Movement

The social learning movement began in the mid 1960s, based primarily upon the research by A. Bandura at Stanford and B. Skinner at Harvard. The essential idea was that people change each other during the course of their interactions. Presumably the changes come about as a function of modeling, punishments, and rewards that are embedded in social exchanges. While this is a common sense notion, the merit of the new work was that it specified methods for studying how these principles worked in the real world. Another important characteristic of these studies was that the ideas were *tested* by collecting data in homes, schools, and other natural settings. While we continue to be interested in what people say about themselves and their lives in interviews and questionnaires, the tenets of social learning theory are based more on observing what families and couples actually *do*. The movement has had a profound impact on the assessment and treatment procedures currently being used by clinical psychologists.

As we applied this new information to the problem of how to help parents retrain their own disturbed children, there were certain themes that appeared repeatedly during treatment. These ideas were written into manuals designed for the parents of the young children that we were treating.(1) The treatment procedures themselves were set down in a written manual (2), and two video tapes.(3) A new book is being prepared that describes the treatment in detail. Years of effort dedicated to helping families change has given us a unique perspective on what families are all about. The combination of field observation plus clinical intervention (referred to as the "research-practitioner" model) leads to a very pragmatic orientation. Ideas or practices which are not supported by data are eventually dropped.

Much of the research being conducted on family processes is scientific; data are constantly collected to check and recheck the ideas. This research is being carried out at a number of sites: in Oregon at the Oregon Social Learning Center and the Oregon Research Institute; in Tennessee with R. Wahler and his colleagues; and more recently in Georgia with R. Forehand, and J. Snyder in Kansas. These research centers share a common goal—to study families by actually going into homes and observing what goes on there. Most of them are also developing treatment programs to help parents change their own families. All of them are part of a broadly-based social learning movement.

The behavioral language and technology that grew out of the work of B. F. Skinner and others is gradually being replaced with a new language and technology. It is an exciting time to be involved in psychological research—the methodology necessary for naturalistic observation is now established, and the tools for building performance models are in hand. This makes it possible for psychology to become an empirical science. The research currently being conducted in our research center, and others, is gradually forming the base for a deeper understanding of how people change as they interact with one another. The term "interactional psychology" refers to this body of knowledge.

Appendix 1 References

1. Patterson, Gerald R. *Living with Children: New Methods for Parents and Teachers*. Champaign, IL: Research Press, revised edition, 1976.
See Also
Patterson, Gerald R. *Families: Applications of Social Learning to Family Life*. Champaign, IL: Research Press, revised edition, 1975.

2. Patterson, Gerald R., Reid, J. B., Jones, R. R., and Conger, R. E. *A Social Learning Approach,* Volume 1: *Families with Aggressive Children*. Eugene, OR: Castalia Publishing Company, 1975.

3. Patterson, Gerald R. *Time Out!* Eugene, OR: Northwest Family and School Consultants, 1984.
See Also
Patterson, Gerald R. *Take A Break*. Eugene, OR: Northwest Family and School Consultants, 1986.

Appendix 2
Short and Long Chores

Short Chores

1. Scrub burner on stove
2. Clean kitchen or bathroom sink
3. Sweep floor
4. Clean toilet bowl
5. Clean mirror in bathroom
7. Empty dishwasher
8. Fold one load of laundry
9. Vacuum carpet in one room
10. Dust one room
11. Wipe down one wall
12. Sweep front or back sidewalk
13. Clean tub or shower
14. Clean out a kitchen cabinet
15. Clean out the refrigerator
16. Scrub floor

17. Polish furniture
18. Water plants
19. Wash car
20. Vacuum car
21. Clean out garbage can
22. Pick up litter in the yard
23. Clean up dog "dirt" in the yard
24. Clean out ashtrays
25. Sweep out garage
26. Wipe down kitchen cabinets
27. Wash dishes
28. Clean out fireplace
29. Bring firewood in
30. Help with ironing

Long Chores

1. Wash windows
2. Clean mold off tiles in shower
3. Clean mold off windows
4. Scrub the outside of pots and pans
5. Rake leaves
6. Pull weeds
7. Chop wood and/or stack it
8. Wash down the outside of the house
9. Clean the rain gutters
10. Mow the lawn and rake it
11. Edge the grass
12. Clean the oven

About the Authors

GERALD R. PATTERSON is the author of two bestselling books for parents: *Living with Children* (over 400,000 copies in print), and *Families* (over 150,000 copies in print). He is also co-author of *The Family Living Series* audiocassette parent training program.

Dr. Patterson is a research scientist at the Oregon Social Learning Center in Eugene, Oregon. His research is focused on the development of social learning theory, delinquency prediction and prevention, treatment strategies for disrupted families, antisocial behavior in children, marital conflict, and observation techniques. He has worked as a family therapist for over 20 years.

Dr. Patterson has earned a world-wide reputation for the excellence of the programmatic research he and his colleagues have carried out over the last 35 years. His most recent professional awards include the Distinguished Scientist Award (Section III, Division 12 of the American Psychological Association, 1982), the Award for Distinguished Contributions in Family Therapy (American Family Therapy Association, 1984), the Distinguished Scientist Award for Applications of Psychology (American Psychological Association, 1985), and the Cumulative Contribution to Research in Family Therapy Award (American Association for Marriage and Family Therapy, 1986). A survey of the Social Science Citation Index by the Institute for Scientific Information in 1982 indicated that Dr. Patterson's research received the most citations in journals dealing with family therapy issues; their conclusion was that Dr. Patterson is one of the most influential researchers in the field of family therapy.

Dr. Patterson is the author of *A Social Learning Approach: Volume 3: Coercive Family Process*. He has written numerous articles for professional journals, and dozens of chapters for textbooks.

MARION S. FORGATCH is co-author of *The Family Living Series* audiocassette parent training program. She is also the senior author of the *Time Out!* videocassette program. Her long-standing interest in the problems and joys of dealing with adolescents began in the late 1960s when she worked with teenagers as a social worker at the YWCA in Honolulu.

Dr. Forgatch joined the group at the Oregon Social Learning Center in 1971 as a research assistant on a project studying marriage conflict. Later, she worked as a therapist with troubled families. Now she combines research and treatment as a research scientist and family therapist at the Oregon Social Learning Center. She has co-authored several observational coding systems in the areas of family problem solving, therapy process, and home observation. Her journal articles and research papers reflect her interests in family problem solving, therapy process, and family adjustment problems associated with separation and divorce.

Dr. Patterson and Dr. Forgatch share an enduring commitment to helping families change. They are currently collaborating on a longitudinal study of the effects of divorce on depression in mothers, and adjustment problems in children from divorced families. Over the past decade they have produced a series of articles and publications teaching normal parents how to change their families.

Jerry and Marion actively use the ideas in this book in designing the social environment in which they live and work. Their lives are a mixture of professional commitment, outdoor recreation, and family activities. About every other weekend they manage to slip away to the mountains and rivers that surround Eugene to make deposits in their interpersonal "bank accounts" with friends and family members. They continue to strive to maintain a balance between the forces of work, play, and love.

Order Form

All orders must be accompanied by a check, money order, or institutional purchase order (VISA and MC also accepted).

Name _____

Address_____

_____

_____

☐ My check is enclosed.
Please charge this order to my ☐ VISA   ☐ MasterCard

_____   _____
card number   exp. date

_____
print signature as it appears on card

NO RISK GUARANTEE: If you are dissatisfied with something you have purchased from us for any reason, the materials may be returned (in new and undamaged condition) within 30 days for a full refund.

Qty.   Amount

_____ **Parents and Adolescents Living Together—Part 1:** _____
       The Basics by Patterson and Forgatch (1-4 copies,
       $11.95 each; 5 + copies, $10.95 each)

_____ **Parents and Adolescents Living Together—Part 2:** _____
       Family Problem Solving by Forgatch and Patter-
       son (1-4 copies, $12.95 each; 5 + copies, $11.95
       each)

* Add $2.50 shipping and handling   Shipping*   _____
per order (U.S. orders); foreign orders,
add $3.50.

                                                     Total   _____

☐ Send current catalog.
☐ Send information about the workbook containing additonal
   homework forms (in a larger format).

Prices are subject to change without notice

Castalia Publishing Company
P.O. Box 1587, Eugene, OR 97440   (503) 343-4433
Your Guide to Better Parenting

Castalia
PUBLISHING   CO.

Order Form

All orders must be accompanied by a check, money order, or institutional purchase order (VISA and MC also accepted).

Name _____

Address_____

_____

_____

☐ My check is enclosed.
Please charge this order to my ☐ VISA   ☐ MasterCard

_____   _____
card number   exp. date

_____
print signature as it appears on card

NO RISK GUARANTEE: If you are dissatisfied with something you have purchased from us for any reason, the materials may be returned (in new and undamaged condition) within 30 days for a full refund.

Qty.   **Amount**

_____   **Parents and Adolescents Living Together—Part 1:**   _____
The Basics by Patterson and Forgatch (1-4 copies, $11.95 each; 5 + copies, $10.95 each)

_____   **Parents and Adolescents Living Together—Part 2:**   _____
Family Problem Solving by Forgatch and Patterson (1-4 copies, $12.95 each; 5 + copies, $11.95 each)

* Add $2.50 shipping and handling   Shipping*   _____
per order (U.S. orders); foreign orders,
add $3.50.

                                             Total   _____

☐ Send current catalog.
☐ Send information about the workbook containing additonal homework forms (in a larger format).

Prices are subject to change without notice

Castalia Publishing Company
P.O. Box 1587, Eugene, OR 97440   (503) 343-4433
Your Guide to Better Parenting

Order Form

All orders must be accompanied by a check, money order, or institutional purchase order (VISA and MC also accepted).

Name _____

Address _____

_____

_____

☐ My check is enclosed.
Please charge this order to my ☐ VISA   ☐ MasterCard

_____   _____
         card number   exp. date

_____
print signature as it appears on card

NO RISK GUARANTEE: If you are dissatisfied with something you have purchased from us for any reason, the materials may be returned (in new and undamaged condition) within 30 days for a full refund.

Qty.   Amount

____ **Parents and Adolescents Living Together—Part 1: The Basics** by Patterson and Forgatch (1-4 copies, $11.95 each; 5 + copies, $10.95 each)   _____

____ **Parents and Adolescents Living Together—Part 2: Family Problem Solving** by Forgatch and Patterson (1-4 copies, $12.95 each; 5 + copies, $11.95 each)   _____

* Add $2.50 shipping and handling   Shipping*   _____
per order (U.S. orders); foreign orders,
add $3.50.

                                       Total   _____

☐ Send current catalog.
☐ Send information about the workbook containing additonal homework forms (in a larger format).

Prices are subject to change without notice

Castalia Publishing Company
P.O. Box 1587, Eugene, OR 97440   (503) 343-4433
Your Guide to Better Parenting